DISTANCE LEARNING

FEATURED ARTICLES

1 **THE KEYS TO ONLINE LEARNING FOR ADULTS: THE SIX PRINCIPLES OF ANDRAGOGY, PART III**
Barbara Zorn-Arnold and Wendy Conaway

7 **PLATO ONLINE CREDIT RECOVERY PROGRAMS FOR MEETING PROMOTIONAL AND GRADUATION REQUIREMENTS**
Nadine P. Anderson

13 **BEYOND THE CLASSROOM-SHOOTING FOR THE STARS: NASA's DIGITAL LEARNING NETWORK**
Michelle Comeau

19 **SUPPORTING STEM SUCCESS WITH ELEMENTARY STUDENTS OF COLOR IN A LOW-INCOME COMMUNITY**
Roxanne Molina, Jia Borror, and Charlene Desir

27 **THE EFFECTIVE INTEGRATION OF TECHNOLOGY INTO SCHOOLS' CURRICULUM**
Charlyque Harris

39 **THE MAJOR ROLE OF FINANCIAL AID GUIDANCE DURING THE ENROLLMENT PROCESS**
Richard Hudnett

43 **A BRIEF HISTORY OF E-LEARNING IN POST-SOVIET ARMENIA**
Varvara Gasparyan

51 **MENTAL HEALTH IN THE ONLINE COLLEGE CLASSROOM: ARE DISTANCE LEARNERS GETTING THE SUPPORT THEY NEED FOR THE CHALLENGES THEY FACE?**
Marianne Raley

57 **ORIENTATION PROGRAMS TO INCREASE RETENTION IN ONLINE COMMUNITY COLLEGE COURSES**
Wendy Robichaud

65 **USDLA AWARD WINNERS**

COLUMNS

ENDS AND MEANS
Motivating the Online Learner Using Keller's ARCS Model   67
—by Natalie B. Milman

TRY THIS
A Miniguide to Mentoring the Online Newbie Educator   73
—by Errol Craig Sull

ASK ERROL!   76
—by Errol Craig Sull

AND FINALLY ...
Flipping, Single Concepts, and Video: So Many New Ideas—Or Are They?   80
—by Michael Simonson

EDITOR
Michael Simonson
simsmich@nova.edu

MANAGING EDITOR
Charles Schlosser
cschloss@nova.edu

ASSISTANT EDITOR
Anymir Orellana
orellana@nova.edu

EDITORIAL ASSISTANT
Khitam Azaiza
azaiza@nova.edu

ASSOCIATION EDITOR
John G. Flores
johnflor@nova.edu

PUBLISHER
Information Age Publishing
11600 North Community
  House Road, Ste. 250
Charlotte, NC 28277
(704) 752-9125
(704) 752-9113 Fax
www.infoagepub.com

ADVERTISING
United States Distance
  Learning Association
76 Canal Street, Suite 301
Boston MA 02114
800-275-5162 x11

EDITORIAL OFFICES
Fischler College of Education
Nova Southeastern
  University
1750 NE 167th St.
North Miami Beach, FL
  33162
954-262-8563
FAX 954-262-3905
simsmich@nova.edu

PURPOSE
Distance Learning, an official publication of the United States Distance Learning Association (USDLA), is sponsored by the USDLA, by the Fischler College of Education at Nova Southeastern University, and by Information Age Publishing. Distance Learning is published four times a year for leaders, practitioners, and decision makers in the fields of distance learning, e-learning, telecommunications, and related areas. It is a professional magazine with information for those who provide instruction to all types of learners, of all ages, using telecommunications technologies of all types. Articles are written by practitioners for practitioners with the intent of providing usable information and ideas for readers. Articles are accepted from authors with interesting and important information about the effective practice of distance teaching and learning.

SPONSORS
The United States Distance Learning (USDLA) is the professional organization for those involved in distance teaching and learning. USDLA is committed to being the leading distance learning association in the United States. USDLA serves the needs of the distance learning community by providing advocacy, information, networking and opportunity.
www.usdla.org

The Fischler College of Education (FCE) of Nova Southeastern University is dedicated to the enhancement and continuing support of teachers, administrators, trainers and others working in related helping professions throughout the world. The school fulfills its commitment to the advancement of education by serving as a resource for practitioners and by supporting them in their professional self development. The college offers alternative delivery systems that are adaptable to practitioners' work schedules and locations. College programs anticipate and reflect the needs of practitioners to become more effective in their current positions, to fill emerging roles in the education and related fields, and to be prepared to accept changing responsibilities within their own organizations.
FCE—NSU
1750 NE 167th St.
North Miami Beach, FL 33162
800-986-3223
www.schoolofed.nova.edu

INFORMATION AGE PUBLISHING
11600 North Community
House Road, Ste. 250
Charlotte, NC 28277
(704) 752-9125
(704) 752-9113 Fax
www.infoagepub.com

SUBSCRIPTIONS
Members of the United States Distance Learning Association receive *Distance Learning* as part of their membership. Others may subscribe to *Distance Learning*.
Individual Subscription: $60
Institutional Subscription: $150
Student Subscription: $40

DISTANCE LEARNING RESOURCE INFORMATION:
Visit http://www.usdla.org/html/resources/dlmag/index.htm
Advertising Rates and Information:
800-275-5162, x11
Subscription Information:
Contact USDLA at
800-275-5162
info@usdla.org

DISTANCE LEARNING is indexed by the Blended, Online Learning and Distance Education (BOLDE) research bank.

DISTANCE LEARNING MAGAZINE
SPONSORED BY THE U.S. DISTANCE LEARNING ASSOCIATION
FISCHLER COLLEGE OF EDUCATION, NOVA SOUTHEASTERN UNIVERSITY
AND INFORMATION AGE PUBLISHING

MANUSCRIPT PREPARATION GUIDELINES

Distance Learning is for leaders, practitioners, and decision makers in the fields of distance learning, e-learning, telecommunications, and related areas. It is a professional journal with applicable information for those involved in providing instruction of all kinds to learners of all ages using telecommunications technologies of all types. Articles are written by practitioners for practitioners with the intent of providing usable information and ideas. Articles are accepted from authors with interesting and important information about the effective practice of distance teaching and learning. No page costs are charged authors, nor are stipends paid. Two copies of the issue with the author's article will be provided. Reprints will also be available.

1. Your manuscript should be written in Microsoft Word. Save it as a .doc file and also as a .rtf file. Send both versions on a flash drive.

2. *Single* space the entire manuscript. Use 12 point Times New Roman (TNR) font.

3. Laser print your paper.

4. Margins: 1" on all sides.

5. Do not use any page numbers, or embedded commands. Documents that have embedded commands, including headers and footers, will be returned to the author.

6. Include a cover sheet with the paper's title and with the names, affiliations and addresses, telephone, and e-mail for all authors.

7. Submit the paper on a flash drive that is clearly marked. The name of the manuscript file should reference the author. In addition, submit two paper copies. A high resolution .jpg photograph of each author is required. Send the flash drive and paper copies to:

Michael R. Simonson,
Editor, Distance Learning
Instructional Design and Technology
Nova Southeastern University
Fischler College of Education
1750 NE 167th Street
North Miami Beach, FL 33162
simsmich@nova.edu
(954) 262-8563

The Manuscript

To ensure uniformity of the printed proceedings, authors should follow these guidelines when preparing manuscripts for submission. DO NOT EMBED INFORMATION. YOUR PAPER WILL BE RETURNED IF IT CONTAINS EMBEDDED COMMANDS OR UNUSUAL FORMATTING INFORMATION.

Word Processor Format
Manuscripts should be written in Microsoft Word.

Length
The maximum length of the body of the paper should be about 3,000 words.

Layout
Top and bottom margins: 1.0"
Left and right margins: 1.0"

Text
Regular text: 12 point TNR, left justified
Paper title: 14 point TNR, centered
Author listing: 12 point TNR, centered
Section headings: 12 point TNR, centered
Section subheading: 12 point TNR, left justified

Do not type section headings or titles in all-caps, only capitalize the first letter in each word. All type should be single-spaced. Allow one line of space before and after each heading. Indent, 0.5", the first sentence of each paragraph.

Figures and Tables
Figures and tables should fit width 6½" and be incorporated into the document.

Page Numbering
Do not include or refer to any page numbers in your manuscript.

Graphics
We encourage you to use visuals—pictures, graphics, and charts—to help explain your article. Graphics images (.jpg) should be included at the end of your paper.

Specialty Books delivers responsive online bookstore solutions customized for your distance learning programs

- A custom bookstore website
- Flexible solutions meet your program needs
- Easy, convenient ordering
- You select student pricing and program revenue
- Accurate, timely fulfillment
- All services at no cost to you

800.446.1365
www.specialty-books.com

Specialty Books®
Your Online Bookstore Partner

Nebraska Book Company

IN UPCOMING ISSUES

Distance Education and Jamaica's Higher Education System	*Patricia Georgia Daley Chin*
Implementing Differentiated Instruction for Online College Writing Courses: Addressing Challenges and Developing Best Practices	*Heather Lunsford and Gretchen Treadwell*
Investigating the Effect of Distance Education System on the Media Literacy of MA Students in Tehran University	*Mosen Keshavarz and Torbat Heydariyeh University of Medical Sciences*
Special Section: Richard Clark Revised: What Health Professionals Say	

The Keys to Online Learning for Adults
The Six Principles of Andragogy, Part III

Barbara Zorn-Arnold and Wendy Conaway

As education leaders, teachers, subject matter experts, and course designers, it is important that we capitalize on students' need to learn, orientation to learning, and motivation to learn in order to support their academic success. In this third installment, we review the remaining three principles of andragogy and offer suggestions for incorporating them into the online classroom. Many adult students return to college after years of pedagogical conditioning, which may make them apprehensive to the openness and self-directedness of andragogical strategies (Forrest & Peterson, 2006). In addition, our mature adult students struggle with balancing work, home, and family. There are ways in which we can keep their spirits and motivation strong so that they can embrace self-directed learning and achieve their goals.

READINESS TO LEARN

Adult students return to school with a wealth of experience and several identities related to the multiple roles they play in life, including parent, employee, commu-

Wendy Conaway,
Ashford University,
8620 Spectrum Center Blvd.,
San Diego, CA. 92123.
Telephone: (858) 776-1379.
E-mail: wendy.conaway@ashford.edu

Barbara Zorn-Arnold,
Ashford University,
8620 Spectrum Center Blvd.,
San Diego, CA. 92123.
Telephone: (858) 776-0796.
E-mail: barbara.zornarnold@ashford.edu

nity volunteer, and leader. Because adults have learned that each role they take on requires new learning and responsibility, they have formed the learning habit of "needing to know" to support a specific role or goal (Knowles, 1984). Moreover, there is a sense of immediacy to fulfill the roles and responsibilities as parent, employee, leader, et cetera that prompts them to seek the learning they need (Cossom & Riches, 1977). The adult students we work with enter college with an eagerness to learn content that has relevance to their immediate goals, which can be career based or something broader, such as making a positive contribution to society. Students are also ready to learn because they have identified gaps in their knowledge and have a sense of what they need to learn in order to achieve their goals. However, some mature adult students are also at high risk for dropping out. If the course content is not immediately obvious, then students may lose motivation, drift, do poorly, and leave school. The risk is particularly great in general education courses, where the content may seem disconnected from students' career goals. In order to improve retention, education leaders and teachers must find ways to demonstrate the relevance and interconnectedness of all subjects.

In our courses, we pay special attention to students' introductions and take notes of their interests, degree program, and intrinsic motivators. The classroom introduction, whether online or on campus, provides a wealth of useful information for instructors. This is where teachers learn why adult students have returned to school, their goals, and factors that drive those goals. Some students return for career advancement, whereas others wish to make a contribution to the world. The factors driving goals are often family. Students will tell us that we wish to be better providers and role models for their children. Others wish to honor their spouses and parents in order to make them proud.

Taking notes on their goals and motivating factors can be used throughout the course in the discussion forum, feedback, or in conversations reminding students of what is important to them and why they have returned to school. Using this information is especially effective in general education courses, where adult learners may struggle with material that appears to be unrelated to their majors. For instance, when teaching a general education course in environmental science, an instructor might ask the follow-up question during a discussion, such as, "How might a stricter air pollution policy affect your job as a hospital administrator?" In this example, the instructor has capitalized on the student's desire to return to school to advance a career in hospital administration and has created a problem-based scenario with immediate application for the student. The instructor has also created meaningful learning that can maintain student engagement and motivation in courses where students may not see a direct relationship with the course and their goals. In addition, it promotes critical thinking by broadening and deepening the students' understanding of how their future career can be impacted and influenced by other factors.

ORIENTATION TO LEARNING

Mature adult students enter college with a readiness to learn focused on supporting their current life situation and fulfilling immediate goals. Readiness to learn is closely tied to orientation to learning, which is a problem-based or performance-based approach to teaching and learning (Forrest & Peterson, 2006). Students seek relevance and immediate application of the content. Orientation to learning is especially engaging for adult students if it is geared toward using knowledge in the workplace and work-related problem solving. Cementing course content with student career development also helps students retain knowledge because the material has an immediate application and meaning for students. Many of our students enjoy problem- and scenario-based assignments as they relate to addressing everyday issues that professionals face in the work place. However, these kinds of activities can also create assessment challenges in the classroom because many work-related problems do not have a single, correct solution. There could be multiple solutions with varying degrees of effectiveness depending on the circumstances. Thus, it is important that instructional strategies emphasize the process of analyzing problems and teaching students to evaluate multiple outcomes.

Educators need to demonstrate to students that the "right" answer is not always as important as the thought process that led to a solution. For example, in one of our courses, a take-home laboratory kit is used to conduct environmental science experiments. Some students become very anxious because they do not know what answer to expect or if they will come up with the "correct" experimental results. In this scenario, it is communicated to students that the assessment focuses on the underlying concepts, completion, and a discussion of the results that were found rather than a specific set of numerical results. Even if the experiment is a disaster, a student can still earn a respectable grade by explaining the process that led to the errors and how they can be corrected. This enhances students' self-confidence and their ability to think independently rather than simply seeking out what is perceived to be the "right" answer.

Another strategy for supporting students' readiness to learn and orientation to learning is to offer students choices in assignments, including choices in subtopics and in format type. Assignment choices appeal to the self-directedness of mature adult students who are ready to learn and eager to apply their learning to their goals. For example, students may have a choice of different subtopics, or formatting options such as writing a paper, developing a poster, publishing an online portfolio, or creating a Prezi or YouSeeU presentation. Other meaningful assignments that appeal to adult learners include community-based projects such as community action planning or a service project assignment (Ames & Diepstra, 2006). Creative assessments allow students to take responsibility for their learning, solve problems that they see as important to their everyday lives, and engage in meaningful work that can benefit the greater good. One challenge for instructors using assignment choices is to ensure that assignment options are equal in rigor and closely support the course learning objectives.

INTRINSIC MOTIVATION

Adult students returning to college may have a different set of motivational factors depending on their age, stage in life, and cognitive interests. Young adults (26–40) may be raising families and are often interested in developing their careers and financial stability. More mature adults (40–65) may have stronger interests in community leadership and advancing to careers that they find meaningful and benefit society. We have had many students tell us that after putting their education on hold to raise their families, they are finally returning to college because they want to set an example for their children or grandchildren, or because they are fulfilling their dream of becoming a teacher, psychologist, environmental advocate, et cetera. A common theme is that these factors are essentially internally driven. In other words, adult students are not returning to college because they were *told* to do so; they are returning to college because they *want* to do so as based on their current or future needs, or desires.

The way in which course content is presented to learners can appeal to the different motivational factors influencing college students. For instance, students with a strong cognitive interest could respond well to emphasis on learning, laboratories, and intellectual discourse. Other students may feel a stronger motivation toward course material that is related to solving problems in the workplace. Many students return to school with a strong desire to make the world a better place. Based on their own personal experiences, they want to contribute to helping others avoid or cope with the problems they themselves endured.

Providing students with engaging and meaningful course materials is another area in which faculty can support students' readiness to learn, orientation for learning, and intrinsic motivation. Online course materials should be engaging and include diverse options such as microvideos, journal articles, newspaper articles, government reports, online simulations, games, interactive tutorials, maps, graphs, and images. It is vital that course materials and assessments directly support both the course learning objectives and students' need to learn from a problem-based approach. However, curriculum strategy should not over emphasize workplace scenarios and career development assignments at the cost of course content and rigor. It is vital to find an instructional balance that cements knowledge with application. This can be accomplished by emphasizing critical thinking tasks as they relate to problem solving and other applications of the course content (Riaz, Bao, Kirwan, Weitl, & Zorn-Arnold, 2015). Classroom materials should be directly related to current events that impact families and careers, include multiple perspectives, and present case studies from both local and foreign areas but still support course learning objectives. For example, in a course on environmental policy, an instructor might include two videos presenting opposing policy viewpoints and ask students to dissect the argument and predict long- and short-term environmental outcomes from each viewpoint. This kind of learning activity supports students' need to address problems, relate policy concepts to environmental outcomes, and prepare them for professional work that has a meaningful impact on society.

ANDRAGOGICAL STRATEGIES AS A GUIDE

Andragogy is a guide to help educators design and implement curriculum in ways that helps students learn their best (Houle, 1996, cited in Merriam, 2001, p. 5). Bedi (2004) points out that andragogy also helps educators identify the challenges that online adult students face and implement learning opportunities that promote self-directedness. By creating learning environments that offer choices in learning and skill development, college educators can appeal to a broad range of adult learning styles and motivational factors. Using andragogical principles are the keys to developing an engaging learning experience for mature adult students. The classroom discussions and assessments should be designed to capitalize on students' need to learn and orientation to learning. Instructors can maintain students' ambition for college by tapping into the intrinsic motivators that students reveal during their introductions. Successful online course design and delivery should cement rigorous course content with relevant problem solving activities that can be immediately applied to adult learners' lives and goals.

REFERENCES

Ames, N., & Diepstra, S. A. (2006). Using intergenerational oral history service-learning projects to teach human behavior concepts: A qualitative analysis. *Educational Gerontology, 32*(9), 721–735.

Bedi, A. (2004). An andragogical approach to teaching styles. *Education for Primary Care, 15*, 93–108.

Cossum, J., & Riches, G. (1977). Dilemmas of the andragogical model in social work education: The Saskatchewan example. *Canadian Journal of Social Work Education, 3*(2), 20–27.

Forrest, S. P., III, & Peterson, T. O. (2006). It's called andragogy. *Academy of Management Learning and Education, 5*(1), 113–122.

Knowles, M. (1984). *Andragogy in action: Applying modern principles of adult learning.* San Francisco, CA: Jossey-Bass.

Merriam, S. B. (2001). Andragogy and self-directed learning: Pillars of adult learning theory. *New Direction for Adult and Continuing Education, 89,* 3–13.

Riaz, S., Bao, M., Kirwan, J., Weitl, J., & Zorn-Arnold, B. (2015). Do students use etextbooks meaningfully? Lessons learned from four online university courses. *Journal of Modern Education, 5*(10), 951–961.

LIVES FOREVER
CHANGED
DOCTOR OF EDUCATION AND MASTER'S DEGREE PROGRAMS
NOVA SOUTHEASTERN UNIVERSITY ABRAHAM S. FISCHLER SCHOOL OF EDUCATION
The Fischler School has long been recognized for excellent online curricula and innovative, flexible delivery options. Our graduate programs are ideal for educational technology professionals who want to expand their leadership skills, improve their ability to manage technology and distance education programs, and explore advancements in educational research and practice. The Fischler School enables school technology leaders to bring about meaningful and lasting change in schools and the world.
Learn more about our master's and doctoral programs in Instructional Technology & Distance Education (ITDE) at fischlerschool.nova.edu/distlearn
NSU NOVA SOUTHEASTERN UNIVERSITY
Abraham S. Fischler School of Education
NCATE
The Standard of Excellence in Teacher Preparation
Connect with us
Nova Southeastern University admits students of any race, color, sexual orientation, and national or ethnic origin.
Nova Southeastern University is accredited by the Southern Association of Colleges and Schools Commission on Colleges to award associate's, baccalaureate, master's, educational specialist, doctorate, and professional degrees. Contact the Commission on Colleges at 1866 Southern Lane, Decatur, Georgia 30033-4097 or call 404-679-4500 for questions about the accreditation of Nova Southeastern University.

Plato Online Credit Recovery Programs for Meeting Promotional and Graduation Requirements

Nadine P. Anderson

INTRODUCTION

The No Child Left Behind Law of 2002 was created to hold schools accountable for the education of their students (Klein, 2015). According to Gordon, to graduate on time a student must complete one grade per year from their freshman through their senior year. If a student is held back at any time during those 4 years, they are not counted as a "graduate" at the time they receive their diploma (Gordon, 2007). Under No Child Left Behind to be counted as a graduate, it must be within that 4-year time span without any holds (Gordon, 2007). Schools were being held accountable for the academic progress that students were achieving (Klein, 2015). It focused on the students they considered to be at risk of failing. Today 1.2 million students drop out of school each year, 26 per second (Dessoff, 2009).

"Nationwide, nearly one third of high school students fail to graduate with a diploma, with an average of 7,000 dropping out every day. The problem is even more severe among African American and Hispanic students, with nearly 50 percent not completing high school on time" (Dessoff, 2009). This is far too many students at risk of failing and in danger of not promoting or not graduating from school this year. Failing just one class can affect whether you will walk the stage on that one night with your friends. What is the solution? For some it is easy, they work hard and they make up the missing credits, for others it is not so easy. For some it is the decision to drop out, and it can affect a person's entire life. A reason a student may drop out of school is due to course failures, emotional problems, life circumstances, boredom, and low self-esteem (Luopa,

Nadine P. Anderson,
Doctoral Student, Nova Southeastern University, P.O. Box 861, Parrish, FL 34219.
Telephone (941) 320-2222.
E-mail: Nadine@parrish-design.com

2010; Franco & Patel, 2011). The failing has placed them off course with their friends and repeating the class has now placed them as a sophomore in a class filled with freshman. This is detrimental to the students' self-esteem; in addition, the failure has them believing they are unable to do this, so why even try. They feel stupid and beaten and believe the easiest solution is to drop out. Life circumstances include teen pregnancy, family struggling, and the student needing to go to work to help pay the bills.

Brady had always been a straight A student through middle school and his first year of high school when school started to get hard. It was his junior year; he was not an A student any more. His grades had dropped to Cs, and Ds, and now he was failing second semester Spanish. As he was finishing the school year, he was a half credit short of becoming a senior and his parents did not know what to do. A conference with his teachers revealed that he had not been turning in any of his assignments and he had turned into the class clown. Brady swore he turned in all his assignments and the teachers lost them all. He felt he would do better in school if he went to the Florida Virtual School for his senior year. Brady started his senior year still a half credit deficient at Florida Virtual School—but was unmotivated to work and 5 weeks into the school year dropped out of school. Brady's scenario is very similar to many other students who drop out but with one exception. Brady got his GED and graduated 6 months before any of his friends and he entered the work force as a short-order cook. On the downside, not all colleges will consider a GED the same as a high school diploma, and only some branches of the military will accept a GED and it could affect him later in life.

Factors that have been associated with a student dropping out of school are based upon four domains: individual, family, school, and community (Rumberger & Lim, 2008). The individual domain deals with students having learning disabilities, emotional disturbance, early adult responsibilities such as working, school performance, school engagement, social attitudes, and behavior (Rumberger & Lim, 2008). The family domain covers socioeconomic status, parental education, family mobility, family size, and family commitment to the school (Rumberger & Lim, 2008). The school domain focuses on achievement, age at retention, and attendance (Rumberger & Lim, 2008). Together, all these play a factor in whether a student drops out of school. In order to keep the student from dropping out we must show the student there is an alternative method. This is where PLATO comes into play.

PLATO

PLATO stands for programmed logic for automatic teaching operations, and was developed in the early 1960s at the University of Illinois by Don Blitzer and Charles Sherwin (Gordon, 2007). PLATO is one of many online programs being utilized by school systems as an alternative method for regaining lost credit for at risk youth. According to Kim Feltner, "credit recovery or credit retrieval is usually defined as an in-school opportunity for students to earn academic credits that they have lost, or are about to lose, by failing a regular course" (Trotter, 2008). There are many schools using credit recovery as an alternative means to promotion in math, science, English, and social studies. Credit recovery is handled in many different ways at different schools. It is even being used at correctional institutions so inmates can earn their high school diploma while incarcerated. Plato is being done face to face, online, and as a blended learning program. Today, the most common method is the online version of PLATO.

PLATO has three components that can be used with credit recovery. The first component is face to face with an online component. The face-to-face class has been used in schools with students who have been in trouble before. Many of the students in this program have been court ordered (Dessoff, 2009). It can be the best way to help students who have "burned many bridges" through academic failure, absenteeism, and disciplinary issues in and out of school" (Dessoff, 2009, p. 44). In order to be accepted into this program, the student and parent must be interviewed and approved by the superintendent of the schools and a member of the board of education (Dessoff, 2009). These students are very far behind in both reading and writing. They need teachers who will work with them; therefore, they spend half the time in the classroom and half the time in the computer lab (Dessoff, 2009). There is a zero tolerance behavior policy for students. In order to stay enrolled in the program, students must attend at least 80% of the classes. Leaving early is considered an absence and a cause for dismissal. Attendance is a huge issue, and only half of the students end up graduating (Dessoff, 2009).

Dillon, a Manatee county teacher, previously worked as an alternative education teacher doing credit recovery in Kenosha County Wisconsin. She worked with students who had dropped out of high school but who wanted to get their high school diploma. Using PLATO face to face with her students, she had much success. Her students ranged in age from 20 to 23 years of age. Prior to beginning this program the students and their parents had to meet with the head of the alternative education program. Here they discussed the requirements required for successful completion of the program and the expectations to stay in the program. Both students and parents had to sign a contract stating they were going to abide by the rules of the program or suffer the consequences that would result (Dillon, personal communication, April 15, 2015). Eligibility entailed the student showing up every morning from 7:30 to 10:00 or every afternoon from 12:30 to 3:00 (Dillon, personal communication, April 15, 2015). Prior to the start of the program, all records were received from the student's prior high school and it was determined ahead of time where they were deficient in credits. The students would sign in upon arrival and go straight to work. The room was silent, there was no camaraderie, and no one knew each other (Dillon, personal communication, April 15, 2015). Teachers worked in pairs with up to 30 students in each room. The PLATO unit came in modules and to pass the student had to have a minimum score of 80% (Dillon, personal communication, April 15, 2015). If students knew the material they could test out and move onto the next module. Students had to score at least 80% on the final assessment to receive the credit (Dillon, personal communication, April 15, 2015).

Florida Virtual School and many other providers offer all-online credit recovery. The nice part about doing credit recovery is this way is that it is done on the students time, at their pace. The student makes his/her schedule and must complete it within 18 weeks. Due to open enrollment, the student can begin the course anytime throughout the school year (Dessoff, 2009). Students can contact teachers from 8 A.M. to 8 P.M. daily, along with e-mail and instant messaging. Teachers are always available if a student needs help. In addition, teachers make monthly support calls to the students and parents to make sure that they are on schedule and to make sure everything is going as planned, as well as discussion-based assessments via the phone (Dessoff, 2009).

One school that has utilized PLATO online is Castle Park Middle School in Chula Vista, California. Here, a large portion of Hispanic students were failing in English and math and were at risk of not being promoted (Washburn, 2004). As a result, PLATO was implemented with the students who were to attend daily sessions (including weekends), with the use of this courseware until the credits were made up. Prior to beginning the PLATO session, a pretest is given to determine the student's ability level (Washburn, 2004). The pretest determines where the student needs to begin in the course. A student is marked exempt in areas they have already mastered (Washburn, 2004). Instruction begins in the area where they need the most assistance or are experiencing the most difficulty. A posttest is given at the end of the session to assess the student's progress and again at the end of the module to determine whether the student has earned the credit back.

Victoria McKnight an 18-year old from New Orleans who attended three high schools before she found one that would meet her needs for her to graduate. She stated, "computer-based courses allow her to work at her own speed and more easily avoid the distractions of classmates" (Carr, 2014, p. 31). She also stated that some of the lessons were very difficult and hard to understand which was very frustrating to her and in those instances; she would prefer to have a regular teacher. The labs do have teachers on staff but the teachers are not always proficient in all the material.

PLATO Hybrid is the last type of credit recovery course. A hybrid course combines both face-to-face and online elements. It is also known as blended learning. The Omaha public schools follow this model. Students go to a lab to do their classwork; if they are stuck, an instructor is there to help them. According to Sachs, "Students go to one of the labs three hours once a week for a semester to regain the credits they need. Depending on their schedules, students can go to the labs at their own schools during regular school hours or to labs at other schools from 3 P.M. to 6 P.M. or 6 P.M. to 9 P.M." (Dessoff, 2009, p. 46). According to the North America Council for Online Learning, the blended approach is the most beneficial to students because it allows extra support to the students by having teachers available for one on one contact (2008). Students that are at risk need this extra support and it provides them with access to technology they normally would not have access to giving them much-needed 21st century skills (North America Council for Online Learning, 2008) According to Susan Patrick, the chief executive officer of North America Council for Online Learning,

> If a student has learned 40% of the material, online credit recovery allows accelerated learning based on competency. If a student is struggling with a lesson, the teacher can focus instruction where the student needs the greatest support. This individualization and personalization allows students to feel a one-to-one connection with their teachers and engages them with the material more thoughtfully. (2008, p. 17)

The blended format allows students to focus the credit recovery help in the area where they need it the most, whether it is one on one with the instructor or it is computer-based instruction.

Dover high school in Dover, Delaware used PLATO with seniors who were in danger of not graduating. These students were disruptive in their classes and were on the way to becoming dropouts before the implementation of PLATO. Without this program, approximately 50 students were in danger of not graduating (Edmentum, 2013). To be a part of this program, students had to be behind in their studies and at least 17 years of age. Classes would met Monday through Thursday for three hours per day. There was a certified teacher in the classroom with the students at all times to offer assistance as needed (Edmentum, 2013).

Some benefits of the PLATO courseware are that it is self-paced, completely online, and students become more competent with the use of technology. PLATO helps to meet a graduation requirement by taking an online class, it keeps distractions at a minimum so the student can stay focused, and students realize they are responsible for making up their own credits (K. Landrigen, personal communication, April 16, 2015). Instruction is individualized and is based upon the student's needs for graduation. Students learn about time management skills and learn about how they can effectively plan for their course work. The students tend to build on their ability to develop higher order thinking skills while increasing their ability to problem solve. For some students online courses may be more engaging than traditional face-to-face classes. In addition, "programs that use online courses can address mobility issues of students who move regularly from one school in the district to another" (North America Council for Online Learning, 2008, p. 15).

Summary

Today, more than 1 million students drop out per year, and approximately one third of the students who graduate do not do so on time (NACOl, 2008). Students without a high school diploma are more likely to be unemployed and work for a lower wages than those who graduated from high school. In addition, not having a high school diploma has been linked to higher crime and higher rates of incarceration (Franco & Patel, 2011). Some students believe that the GED is a viable option to dropping out and, in the past, it was. The GED was created in 1942 at the request of the military as a way to "demonstrate competency and move on to a new career or further education" (LaPonsie, 2012, para. 4). However, today some branches of the military will not accept a GED. The fast food industry also wants its employees to have a high school diploma (Weissman, 2013).

Students should be encouraged to get their diplomas. There are multiple options available for credit recovery so they may do so. Credit recovery can be used to meet the individual needs of these students.

These are the face to face, online and hybrid. PLATO is just one of the many credit recovery systems available today. Through credit recovery, students are learning to become competent with technology. They are learning to become self-directed and responsible for their own learning. Students are now realizing that in order for them to graduate it is their responsibility. No one is going to do it for them, but there is support there to help them when and if they need it.

On the bright side, graduation rates are on the rise and it is expected by the year 2020 that 90% of the student population will be graduating with a high school diploma (Balfanz & Gomperts, 2013).

References

Balfanz, R., & Gomperts, J. (2013). What you won't hear at high school graduation. Retrieved from http://www.cnn.com/2013/06/06/opinion/balfanz-high-school-graduation/

Carr, S. (2014). Credit recovery hits the mainstream. *Education Next, 14*(3), 30–36

Dessoff, A. (2009). Reaching graduation with recovery. *District Administration, 45*(9), 43–48.

Edmentum. (2013). Dover High School – PLATO courseware & Edoptions academy. Retrieved from http://www.edmentum.com/resources/success-stories/dover-high-school-plato-courseware-edoptions-academy-dover-de

Franco, M. S., & Patel, N. H. (2011). An interim report on a pilot credit recovery program in a large, suburban Midwestern high school. *Education, 132*(1), 15–27.

Klein, A., (2015). No child left behind: An overview. Retrieved from http://www.edweek.org/ew/section/multimedia/no-child-left-behind-overview-definition-summary.html

Gordon, R. (2007). *An analysis of at-risk student achievement in a PLATO credit recovery course* (Unpublished doctoral dissertation). University of Mississippi, Oxford, MS. (UMI No. 3329544)

LaPonsie, M., (2012). Should you get a high school diploma or a GED. Retrieved from http://www.onlineschools.com/in-focus/

should-you-get-a-high-school-diploma-or-a-aged

Luopa, P. E. (2010). *Heading toward the finish line: Effects of PLATO online courses on credit recovery* (Unpublished doctoral thesis). Capella University, Minneapolis, MN.

Rumberger, R., & Lim, S.A., (2008). Why students drop out of school: A review of 25 years of research. California Dropout Research Project, UC Santa Barbara, Gevirtz Graduate School of Education. Retrieved from http://www.slocounty.ca.gov/Assets/CSN/PDF/Flyer+-+Why+students+drop+out.pdf

Trotter, A. (2008). Online options for credit recovery widen. *Education Week, 27*(38), 1–2.

Washburn, J. (2004). Credit-recovery program helps at-risk students meet promotional requirements. *T.H.E. Journal, 32*(1), 42–44.

Weissman, J., (2013). More than a quarter of fast-food workers are raising a child. Retrieved http://www.theatlantic.com/business/archive/2013/08/more-than-a-quarter-of-fast-food-workers-are-raising-a-child/278424/

Beyond the Classroom, Shooting for the Stars
NASA's Digital Learning Network

Michelle Comeau

INTRODUCTION

The National Aeronautics and Space Administration's (NASA) Digital Learning Network (DLN) commenced in 2003 with three sites in the United States for students and educators to connect with NASA scientists via web or videoconferencing to enhance student engagement and understanding of scientific concepts through participation in themed programs used to supplement classroom curricula (Cherry & Talley, 2013). Since then, seven more sites have opened in the United States, allowing for more than a million student-scientist interactions per year (Moseley & Brown, 2013). Evolution of the DLN includes the formation of Explorer Schools, NASA TV, and a powerful presence on social media.

EVOLUTION OF NASA'S DLN

The DLN is a means to incorporate the learning cycle of the 5 Es—"engage, explore, explain, elaborate, and evaluate" (Bybee, 1997)—through programmed scientific agendas broadcast through interactive conferencing between NASA scientists and K–16 classrooms in the United States. The learning cycle of the 5 Es is an inquiry-based pedagogy promoted by NASA curriculum designers and scientists to interact with programs in an effort to address each area of the 5E cycle. The cyclic nature of the learning model supports retention and comprehension of material (Cavallo & Laubach, 2001). The specific 5E model was created in the mid-1980s in hopes of increased learning through the addition of engagement and evaluation within the cycle (Cherry & Talley, 2013). NASA seemingly successfully incorporated the 5E-model into distance education curriculum.

Since 2013, the DLN has evolved to include increased interactions beyond the classroom with live 24-hour per day interactions between NASA scientists, sometimes live from the International Space Station, and any student or educator inter-

Michelle Comeau,
137 Hunt Hill Rd.,
Rindge, NH 03461.
(603) 899-7670.
E-mail: mc1953@nova.edu

Table 1. Summary of the Biological Sciences Curriculum Study 5E Instructional Model

Phase	Summary
Engagement	The teacher or a curriculum task accesses the learners' prior knowledge and helps them become engaged in a new concept through the use of short activities that promote curiosity and elicit prior knowledge. The activity should make connections between past and present learning experiences, expose prior conceptions, and organize students' thinking toward the learning outcomes of current activities.
Exploration	Exploration experiences provide students with a common base of activities within which current concepts (i.e., misconceptions), processes, and skills are identified and conceptual change is facilitated. Learners may complete lab activities that help them use prior knowledge to generate new ideas, explore questions and possibilities, and design and conduct a preliminary investigation.
Explanation	The explanation phase focuses students' attention on a particular aspect of their engagement and exploration experiences and provides opportunities to demonstrate their conceptual understanding, process skills, or behaviors. This phase also provides opportunities for teachers to directly introduce a concept, process, or skill. Learners explain their understanding of the concept. An explanation from the teacher or the curriculum may guide them toward a deeper understanding, which is a critical part of this phase.
Elaboration	Teachers challenge and extend students' conceptual understanding and skills. Through new experiences, the students develop deeper and broader understanding, more information, and adequate skills. Students apply their understanding of the concept by conducting additional activities.
Evaluation	The evaluation phase encourages students to assess their understanding and abilities and provides opportunities for teachers to evaluate student progress toward achieving the educational objectives.

Source: Bybee et al. (2006).

ested in NASA research, missions, and discoveries. While some programs have changed or have been eliminated, such as the Explorer School Programs, where schools within 26 districts were essentially adopted by NASA, regardless of their participation in the DLN, and visited by NASA scientists and education professionals to train teachers how to teach science, technology, engineering, and mathematics (STEM) curricula, some programs, such as NASA TV, have evolved to engage students and citizens alike to live weekly programming (NASA, 2016b). Social media has also blossomed in such a way several scientific agendas are addressed in real time by several scientists and any person can communicate and ask scientists questions any time of day.

DIGITAL LEARNING NETWORK

The Digital Learning Network was fully operational in 2004 (Loston, Steffen, & McGee, 2005). The mission was to connect educators and students to NASA scientists in real time, allowing for student-expert interaction and collaboration. Videoconferencing allows students and scientists to connect using the Internet, enabling both locations to hear and see each other in real time (Pringle, Klosterman, Milton-Brkich, & Hayes, 2010). Hopper (2014) states, "It is possible through videoconferencing and global projects to enhance learning and bring the world to the classroom for all age levels" (p. 88).

NASA seeks to engage students though scientific inquiry, fostering long-term affinity for STEM programs in students around the globe. NASA has 10 operational centers. The centers provided several different programs educators choose to use as supplements to their classroom curricula. Educators would essentially front load, or pre-educate, the students on the topic and then interact with scientists to ask questions and further their understanding of the program content, sometimes scientists would even take students on guided virtual tours or field trips and even live launchings of the space shuttle (Cherry & Talley, 2013). This interaction is critical in learning and cognitive development (Sharan, 1980). Videoconferencing allows for students that may not typically be able to attend a tour in person, nor be able to gain exposure to this type of learning due to living in rural, remote areas (Motamedi, 2001) to experience learning beyond the typical classroom. For instance, the Astronomical Society of the Pacific partnered with NASA to create a national network of amateur astronomy club members to allow students to look through their [scientists'] personally owned telescopes (Manning et al., 2008). Schools unable to receive telescopes are able to connect via the Internet as well, "Electronic access to computer-controlled telescopes equipped with digital cameras can solve some of these difficulties by enabling students and their teachers to access Internet-controllable telescopes, and consult more readily with experts" (Stencel, Harland, Hannahoe, Bisque, & Rice, 2002, p. 719).

EXPLORER SCHOOLS

One year after the premiere of the DLN, NASA began adopting schools throughout the United States that were lacking the means to provide certain STEM programs typically due to financial and location limitations (NASA, 2013a). The schools entered into a 3-year contract with NASA, and NASA provided funding for the schools to purchase equipment, such as telescopes, upgrade technology, and also provide visitations from educational experts to train educators in STEM curricula and resources (Moseley & Brown, 2013; NASA, 2013a).

NASA's 10-year anniversary of the Explorer School program was highly celebrated on the NASA website; however, there is a deficit in the literature as to the effectiveness of the Explorer School programs. Several schools identify themselves as NASA Explorer Schools, even though the program ceased in 2013 and has not been reestablished (NASA, 2013a). More research is necessary to understand the issues that determined its culmination. It is clear from the *2015–2017 Education Implementation Plan* that the drive to educate students at a distance has not ended (NASA, 2016a). NASA is still dedicated to engaging students from all walks of life, in hopes of inspiring dissemination of knowledge for generations.

NASA TV AND SOCIAL MEDIA

Students, educators, and global citizens can now stay tuned with NASA missions and discoveries in real time outside of the DLN and Explorer School programs. NASA has created its own television station, NASA TV, where scheduled programming and live webcasts can be viewed any time of the day from the NASA website. During live programming, interaction with scientists can be conducted via e-mail or social media. In fact, social media has taken on its own identity within NASA, as scientists are online every minute via Twitter, Facebook, Instagram, and various other social networks. Four cameras are set up on the International Space Station filming Earth live from space in celebration of Earth Day 2016. The Environmental Research and Visualization System, a system photographing Earth from the International Space Station, uses this continuous photography of Earth to aid countries experiencing natural disasters around the globe in real time, distance education at its best.

Other ways to stay informed in real time are reading online blogs from NASA scientists and reporters or even joining a NASA Social, "a program to provide opportunities for NASA's social media followers to learn

Source: Retrieved from nasa.gov/explorerschools

Figure 1. NASA Explorer Schools.

Source: 2016 photo by Michelle Comeau.

Figure 2. 5E instructional model, "Inquiry Scholar Showcase," Rindge, NH.

and share information about NASA's missions, people, and programs. NASA Social is the next evolution in the agency's social media efforts" (NASA, 2013b).

BEYOND THE CLASSROOM

Since 2003, NASA has reached beyond the classroom; they have held to their mission, to "inspire a generation of explorers." They try new avenues to engage students, citizens, and educators, and if one avenue does not seem to meet all criteria of the 5Es, they continue to evolve, addressing inquiry throughout the universe and sharing their expertise with all of us.

REFERENCES

Bybee R. W. (1997). *Achieving scientific literacy*. Portsmouth, NH: Heinemann.

Bybee, R. W., Taylor, J. A., Gardner, A., Van Scotter, P., Carlson Powell, J., Westbrook, A., & Landes, N. (2006). *The BSCS 5E instructional model: Origins, effectiveness, and applications* [Executive summary]. Colorado Springs, CO: Biological Sciences Curriculum Study.

Cavallo, A., & Laubach T. (2001). Students' science perceptions and enrollment decisions in differing learning cycle classrooms. *Journal of Research in Science Teaching, 38*(9), 1029–1062.

Cherry, G., & Talley, D. (2013). Reaching beyond the conventional classroom: NASA's Digital Learning Network. In M. Simonson. (Ed.), *Distance education: Statewide, institutional, and international applications of distance education: Readings from the pages of Distance Learning journal* (pp. 121–127). Charlotte, NC: Information Age.

Hopper, S. B. (2014). Bringing the world to the classroom through videoconferencing and project-based learning. *TechTrends, 58*(3), 78–89. doi:10.1007/s11528-014-0755-4

Loston, A., Steffen, P., & McGee, S. (2005). NASA education: Using inquiry in the classroom so that students see learning in a whole new light. *Journal of Science Education and Technology, 14*(2), 147–156.

Manning, J., Gurton, S., Gibbs, M., Zevin, D., Berendsen, M., & Fraknoi, A. (2008). Intermediary astronomy: Education through the leveraging of networks, partnerships and intermediaries at the Astronomical Society of the Pacific. *Communication Astronomy with the Public, 1,* 310.

Moseley, C., & Brown, L. (2013). Impact of participation in NASA's Digital Learning Network on science attitudes of rural mid-level students. *Electronic Journal of Science Education, 17*(3), 1–35.

Motamedi, V. (2001). A critical look at the use of videoconferencing in United States distance education. *Education, 122*(2), 386.

National Aeronautics and Space Association. (2013a). Digital Learning Network. Retrieved from www.nasa.gov/dln

National Aeronautics and Space Association. (2013b). Education. Retrieved from www.nasa.gov/education

National Aeronautics and Space Association. (2016a). NASA education implementation plan. Retrieved from www.nasa.gov/explorerschools

National Aeronautics and Space Association. (2016b). NASA TV. Retrieved from http://www.nasa.gov/multimedia/nasatv/

Pringle, R., Klosterman, M., Milton-Brkich, K., & Hayes, L. (2010, Summer). Collaborative distance learning. *Science and Children,* 52–56.

Sharan, S. (1980). Cooperative learning in small groups: Recent methods and effects on achievement, attitudes, and ethnic relations. *Review of Educational Research, 50,* 241–271.

Stencel, R., Harland, H., Hannahoe, R., Bisque, S., & Rice, M. (2002). The Student Telescope Network (STN) experiment. *Bulletin of the American Astronomical Society, 34,* 719.

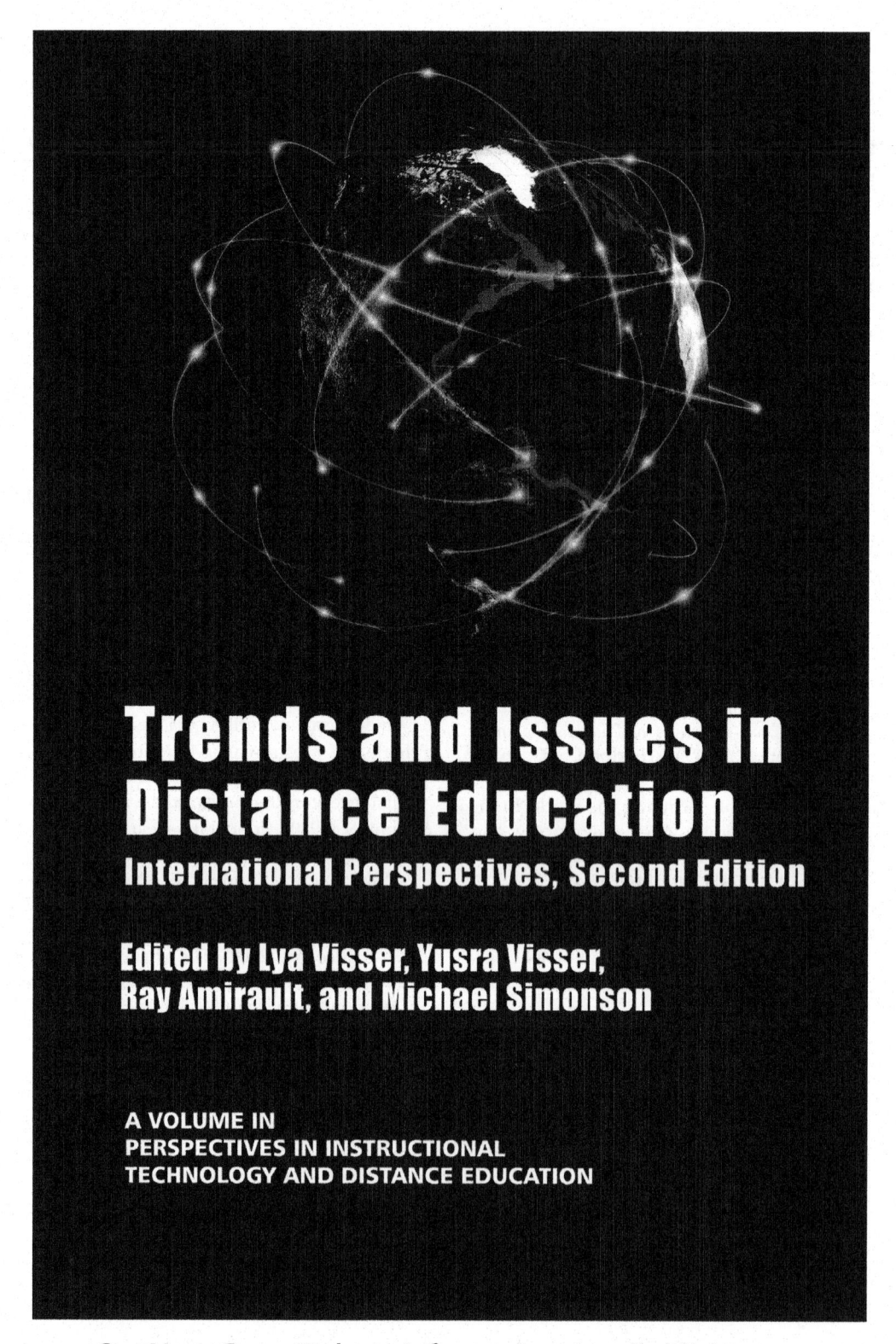

Trends and Issues in Distance Education
International Perspectives, Second Edition

Edited by Lya Visser, Yusra Visser, Ray Amirault, and Michael Simonson

A VOLUME IN
PERSPECTIVES IN INSTRUCTIONAL
TECHNOLOGY AND DISTANCE EDUCATION

Get Your Copy Today—Information Age Publishing

Supporting STEM Success With Elementary Students of Color in a Low-Income Community

Roxanne Molina, Jia Borror, and Charlene Desir

INTRODUCTION

In low-income communities of color with limited social capital and educational resources, school is not often a space of liberation but rather continued marginalization unless there are active and conscious efforts to teach and learn in a creative context that goes beyond the low expectations for children living in poverty (Pigza, 2005). Social justice is essential to foster an educational system that benefits all who participate. The educational structure is not limited to those who work in the school and the families they serve. Professors of education are also part of this expanded community and play a significant role in training the pool of education workers who need to develop and advance their students' critical thinking and academic relevancy to break the cycles of academic

Roxanne Molina,
Assistant Professor and Assessment Coordinator, Abraham S. Fischler College of Education, Nova Southeastern University, 1750 N.E. 167 Street, North Miami Beach, FL 33162.
Telephone: 954-262-8548.
E-mail: rmolina1@nova.edu

Jia Borror,
Assistant Professor, Abraham S. Fischler College of Education, Nova Southeastern University, 1750 NE 167th Street, North Miami Beach, FL 33162.
Telephone: (954) 262-8507.
E-mail: jb239@nova.edu

neglect that perpetuates limited access toward liberation for children of color living in poverty caused by segregation.

In an effort to reconnect to children living in low income communities near NSU, professors of education partnered with a local public school to better understand the growing cognitive needs of one of the poorest elementary schools in the state of Florida. NSU began as an alternative education graduate school and has a history in the creative and inclusive building of education pioneers. The school has since evolved into various departments in many academic fields; nonetheless, the core of its philosophy still resides in the college of education. Professors help to shape the next generation of educators, but at the same time are often removed from the children who ultimately should benefit from their expertise in the field of education. How often do professors go back to the classroom and truly engage young people in theories of learning toward an understanding of education as a tool of liberation?

Charlene Desir,
Associate Professor, Abraham S. Fischler College of Education, Nova Southeastern University, 1750 NE 167th Street, North Miami Beach, FL 33162.
Telephone: (954) 262-8488.
E-mail: cdesir@nova.edu

Having had this opportunity, the research team decided to create a space of learning and teaching to a group of children in a nearby low income community utilizing a science, technology, engineering, and mathematics (STEM) lens. Hillside Elementary School (pseudonym) serves a low-socioeconomic status (SES) population in suburban Broward County, Florida. Of the 608 students enrolled in grades pre-K–5, 96% are on free or reduced lunch. Additionally, the school serves a predominately minority population, with 91.7% of the students identifying as Black/African American and 5.42% as Hispanic. In 2013, Hillside Elementary received an F grade on the Florida statewide assessment, the Florida Comprehensive Assessment Test, and was identified as a FOCUS-D school by the Elementary and Secondary Education Act. Hillside Elementary is a Title I School that failed to make Adequate Yearly Progress for the last 2 years and has been in the bottom 20% of all schools in the state of Florida based on the 2013–2014 Florida Comprehensive Assessment Test results.

Why STEM?

STEM is the term that has come to symbolize a national need for educational reform in the science, technology, engineering, and mathematics disciplines. This focus has developed to address the growing concern that the United States is failing to prepare individuals to compete with their international counterparts in the 21st century global market. According to the Report from the President's Council of Advisors on Science and Technology (2012), the United States will need to educate an additional 1 million STEM professionals over the next decade to maintain its global leadership position and meet the economic challenges of this century. In order to fill these positions, the United States will need to recruit STEM talent across all student groups.

While many students begin their education with a positive perception of the STEM disciplines and the talent needed to pursue and succeed in STEM careers, STEM talent attrition occurs amongst both women and people of color. This is concerning as the U.S. Census Bureau (2009) reports people of color will comprise almost 50% of the U.S. population by 2050 and are currently underrepresented as U.S. STEM discipline majors. The United States cannot afford to lose the potential contributions of people of color as it struggles to maintain its position as a global innovative leader.

THE STEM PROJECT

This year-long partnership with Hillside Elementary began by providing a 1-week professional development institute that included a segment on strategies for addressing STEM content through STEM Design Challenges, a project-based approach to engaging students in the interdisciplinary learning of the STEM disciplines. The institute provided the opportunity for the research team to get to know the Hillside faculty and discuss their current pedagogical strategies for addressing STEM. As is typical in many schools, the research team learned the disciplines were being taught in isolation and the current curriculum did not include opportunities for students to engage in projects such as the STEM Design Challenges. However, as the research team began to expand interactions with the teachers, they became very concerned that in this particular school, in response to perceived student behavior issues, the pedagogical strategies being used were limited to direct instruction with very few opportunities for students to engage in any activity that promoted collaboration, creativity, communication, and critical thinking amongst students. Given the need to develop these skills in students, the research team became very concerned.

In response to this concern, the research team decided to create a learning space that would promote collaboration among Hillside instructional coaches, fourth- and fifth-grade faculty, NSU university faculty across colleges, and community partners, to develop STEM Design Challenges that would align with STEM content standards and focus on identified areas of weaknesses as determined through analysis of quarterly data assessments. To begin the process, as professors with expertise in STEM, elementary education, and multicultural studies, the research team met with Hillside Elementary instructional coaches for mathematics and science to plan the first STEM project for fifth grade. This first STEM project focused on aviation and was designed to target science and mathematics standards that fifth grade students had not mastered based on the last quarter assessment. Once created, the instructional coaches then shared the project with the fifth grade faculty. Fifth grade faculty implemented the project and then participated in planning the next design challenge, which focused on marine pollution, with the fourth grade teachers.

STEM PLAN, DESIGN, CHECK, SHARE

Each design challenge was built around the elementary design cycle of plan, design, check, and share. University faculty along with the Hillside Elementary instructional coaches and eventually Grade 5 and 4 teachers, developed a STEM journal distributed to each student that included activities to address each of the design cycle phases. During the plan phase, students were asked to analyze and write about readings related to the theme (e.g., aviation, marine, etc.) that were differentiated according to student reading level. These readings were selected purposefully to help guide student thinking related to the design challenge. Part of the plan phase were multiple activities and

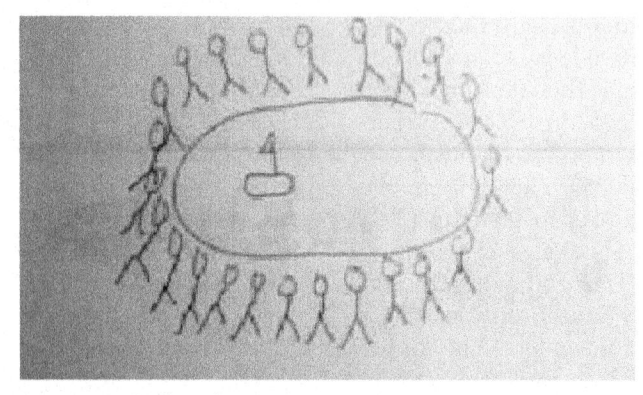

Figure 1. Student drawing.

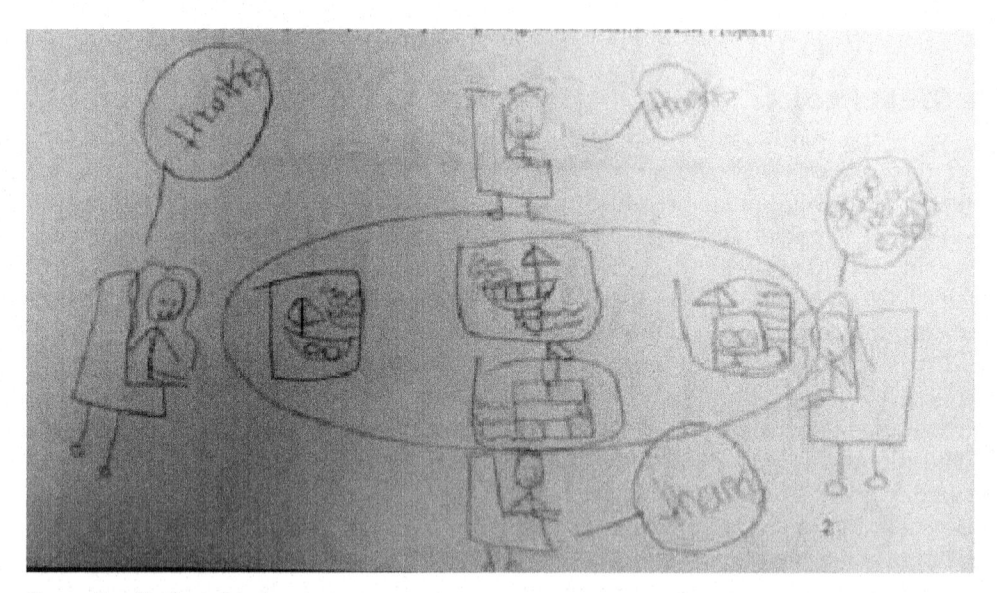

Figure 2. Student drawing.

investigations that addressed the science and mathematics content needed to complete the design challenge. Additionally, students used iPads to engage in digital apps that were selected to align with the science and mathematics content, and as a last stage of the plan phase, students created their own individual prototype drawings.

During the design phase, students discussed the strengths and weaknesses of their individual prototype drawings and then collaboratively decided on a group design. Students created their prototypes based on the selected design. As part of the check phase, students tested whether their prototype met the constraints of the design challenge. If needed, students returned to the plan or design phase to adjust their prototype to meet the design challenge. One student said, "I learned that when you draw out your plan, if it doesn't work, then try again." Lastly, students shared their final designs with the class along with any challenges encountered during the phases.

FOUR CS DEVELOPMENT

According to the Partnership for 21st Century Learning (2011), students need to move beyond the basics and embrace the four Cs, otherwise known as "superskills": collaboration, communication, creativity, and critical thinking. All of these skills were embedded into the STEM Design Challenges and provided students with a new way to learn about science, technology, and math. Students indicated that they "liked helping my friends and my teammates," "had a great experience building the boat," and "made something out of nothing." Rather than learning the subjects separately, science, technology, engineering, and math were integrated into a marine project in which students were required to research and then work collaboratively to design a boat made of recycled materials. Students had to come up with creative designs for their boats and use critical thinking skills when determining which materials would be able to hold the most weight. Two students drew pictures that (1) expressed the community building and communal learning context of the project and (2) expressed thanks and gratitude for the collaborative learning experience.

INTERACTIONS WITH COMMUNITY PARTNERS

Embedded in each of the STEM Design Challenges were opportunities for the students to interact with mentors from the community. The research team organized a group of 10 high school seniors from University School, a K–12 private school on NSU's campus, who volunteered to work one on one with students every Tuesday and Thursday for 2 hours from January through June. The tutoring was focused on all subjects, with a strong focus on reading and math. Additionally, there were two volunteers from America Reads/America Counts who supported Hillside Elementary students once a week for 2 hours for most of the academic year starting in the fall. An intern of color from NSU was placed in one of the Hillside Elementary classrooms to work with students. Additionally, two graduate students from the NSU Guy Harvey Oceanographic Center came to the school to present information on marine pollution, recycling, and career opportunities for the future. This enabled students to make real life connections with the topics and standards that were being covered in class.

The research team also included guest speakers in STEM fields that gave students an opportunity to ask questions about specific topics of interest and provided them with information about community events they could attend with their families. Many of the students were amazed when they learned about the amount of time it takes for items that people throw away to break down in landfills. They also learned about the different things they could do to take care of the earth and the oceans. The graduate students provided their contact information for teachers and students at Hillside Elementary in an effort to establish a partnership for future collaborative projects and presentations.

As a culminating classroom experience, students learned how to use digital storytelling to reflect on the STEM Design Challenge and share their experiences. One of the university professors spent time in the classroom teaching students how to create a story using PowerPoint. Students worked in their collaborative groups to create a final product to present to the class at the end of the year using the 21st century skill of communication. Fourth and fifth grade students also had the opportunity to visit and learn about the Everglades on an airboat tour at the end of the marine STEM Design Challenge. During the field trip experience students were guided by a captain through sawgrass and cattails for a 30-minute airboat ride to learn more about the ecosystem of the Everglades. They were able to see the native and exotic plants and animals that live in their natural habitat. The field trip also included several wildlife exhibits including reptiles, tortoises, peacocks, a panther, and other small mammals. It was the first time many of the students had an opportunity to visit the Everglades, even though the school was less than an hour away. One of the advantages of students participating in the STEM Design Challenge was that students were able to interact with new community partners that were not previously involved at the school.

CONCLUSION

Engaging poor children of color requires not only an understanding of educational theory, but also a recognition of using education as a tool of liberation. This was accomplished at Hillside Elementary School by expanding educational opportunities through a creative process of engagement involving STEM Design Challenges. The challenges encouraged students to interact with intergenerational partners in developing a comprehensive understanding of STEM content. Students were provided opportunities to learn the STEM disciplines through an integrated approach, interact with community members and experts in the STEM fields, and experience STEM in real-life contexts. This allowed students to learn STEM concepts in an authentic way by interacting with others and developing an understanding of how STEM plays a role in their daily lives.

To evaluate the effectiveness of this partnership, issues of equity and access were important lenses to consider. As professors of education responsible for developing future teachers, it is imperative to also have them analyze the various communities and needs that they will serve. Not only was Hillside in a financially impoverished community, there was also a label of major student behavioral problems. These two stigmas played a significant role in the lack of academic resources provided, the low expectations of the students, and the approach to learning. Interestingly, STEM provided greater relevance to these students as they looked at their community not as lacking, but overflowing with all sorts of materials and people that contribute to the larger STEM project needs for the future of the world. They became present in the conversation, having exposure and the opportunity to actively engage in conversation, activities, and field trips to further understand and comprehensively make meaning of STEM to their respective academic and social realities. There were no behavioral issues; they engaged respectfully as the research team engaged them respectfully. There was not a stigma of poverty as a lens; they were simply children of color gifted with the thirst to learn in a context of relevancy, community, and support. As faculty of academic privilege, the research team learned from the students simply that teachers have not done enough to engage their strengths, gifts and abilities. It is an obligation to be vigilant in university classrooms and in the K–12 school community to be agents and partners in social justice learning as a tool of liberation for all children.

After participating in the STEM Design Challenges, results from the annual statewide science assessment revealed fifth grade students' scores at Hillside Elementary School increased for the first time in several years. With an approximate 12% increase from the previous year's scores, teachers and administrators were thrilled and energized. The school principal said, "The experiences provided by the faculty at NSU were invaluable to our learners and our staff. Their mentorship, leadership, and friendship built a relationship that has provided a wonderful foundation for our school to move forward in educating our children." A requirement of social justice teaching is that teachers approach instruction in ways that support the active, engaged learning of all students. Additionally, teachers need to incorporate course content relevant to students' lives, including both students' experiences and the communities in which they live (Brown & Brown, 2011).

REFERENCES

Brown, K. D., & Brown, A. L. (2011). Teaching K–8 students about race: African Americans, racism, & the struggle for social justice in the U.S. *Multicultural Education, 19*(1), 9–13.

National Research Council. (2011). *Successful STEM education: A workshop summary.* Washington, DC: The National Academy Press.

Partnership for 21st Century Learning. (2015). *The 4Cs research series.* Retrieved from www.p21.org

Pigza, J. M. (2005). *Teacher seeks pupil—Must be willing to change the world: A phenomenological study of professors teaching for social justice.* Doctoral dissertation, University of Maryland.

President's Council of Advisors on Science and Technology. (2012). Engage to excel: Producing one million additional college graduates with degrees in science, technology, engineering, and mathematics. Retrieved from https://www.whitehouse.gov/administration/eop/ostp/pcast/docsreports

U.S. Census Bureau. (2009). National population projections. Retrieved from http://www.census.gov/prod/1/pop/profile/95/2_ps.pdf

RICHARD E. CLARK, EDITOR

LEARNING From MEDIA

■ Arguments, Analysis, and Evidence, Second Edition ■

Foreword by Michael Simonson
Charles Schlosser and Michael Simonson, Series Editors
A VOLUME IN PERSPECTIVES IN INSTRUCTIONAL TECHNOLOGY AND DISTANCE LEARNING

Get Your Copy Today—Information Age Publishing

The Effective Integration of Technology Into Schools' Curriculum

Charlyque Joy Harris

Introduction

Technology has become a fundamental part of our daily lives, being infused into entertainment, business, workforce, and educational environments. Technology is used throughout the world for gathering information, keeping records, creating proposals, constructing knowledge, performing simulations to develop skills, distance learning, and global collaboration for lifelong learning and work (Kimble, 1999). Today's educators are under great pressure to provide 21st century students with a quality education based on 21st century standards. Those standards include providing students with the technological and informational skills needed to compete in an ever-changing, technology-driven world.

According to Hamilton, technology should be integrated into curricula to enhance learning in content areas (2007). In order for technology integration to be effective, technology should be a fundamental part of the classroom, allowing students to be able to select technology resources to help them to "obtain information in a timely manner, analyze and synthesize information, and present it professionally" (Hamilton, 2007, p. 3).

Effective technology integration into schools' curricula has the ability to improve student learning outcomes (Hamilton, 2007). Students need technological and informational skills to compete in the 21st century. According to The Partnership for 21st Century Skills (2008) the four standards of 21st century skills are communication, collaboration, critical thinking, and creativity. Technology-enhanced learning experiences may also help student develop 21st century competencies such as information, technology and media literacies, critical thinking, communication and leadership skills, and innovativeness (Aslan, 2015). The International Society for Technology in Education was founded on the principle of preparing students to compete

Charlyque Joy Harris, Technology Education and Engineering Teacher, J. E. Richards Middle School, 3555 Sugarloaf Parkway, Lawrenceville, GA 30044. Telephone: (770) 995-7133. E-mail: Charlyque_Harris@gwinnett.k12.ga.us

WHAT ARE 21ST CENTURY SKILLS? THESE 4 C'S:

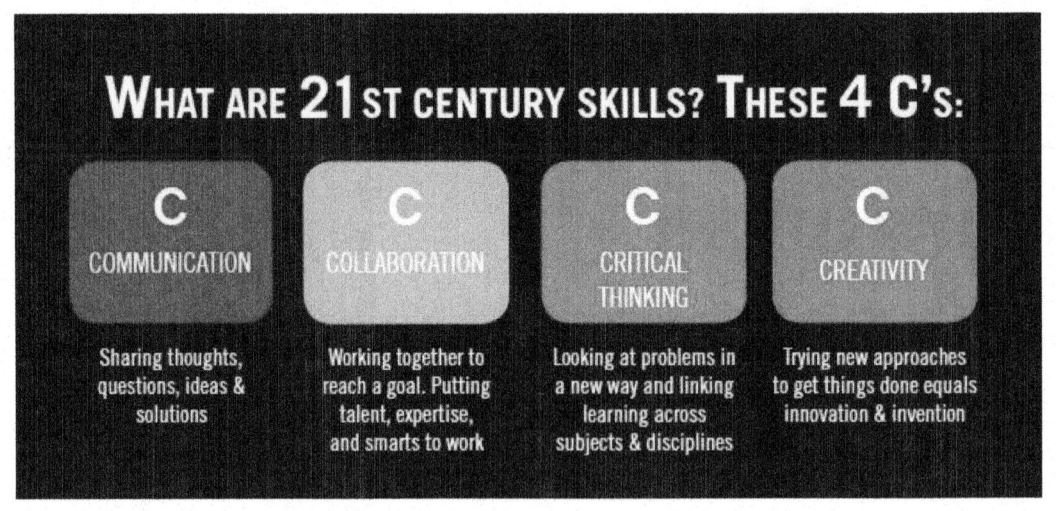

C COMMUNICATION — Sharing thoughts, questions, ideas & solutions

C COLLABORATION — Working together to reach a goal. Putting talent, expertise, and smarts to work

C CRITICAL THINKING — Looking at problems in a new way and linking learning across subjects & disciplines

C CREATIVITY — Trying new approaches to get things done equals innovation & invention

Figure 1. Description of the 4 Cs of 21st century skills.

in a technology-driven world by providing them with the skills to be technology literate.

CONTROVERSY

The educational community has not completely bought into the idea of technology integration; in fact technology integration has caused a large amount of controversy. At the heart of this debate are Richard Clark and Robert Kozma. Clark (2012) describes media as "mere vehicles that deliver instruction but do not influence student achievement" (p. 2). Kozma counters Clark's view by asking the question "what are the actual and potential relationships between media and learning?" (Kozma, 1994, p. 1). Clark asserts that learning outcomes are influenced by instructional design. Kozma counters that different media, under certain conditions produces positive learning outcomes. Although Clark initially expressed his views in 1983 and Kozma countered in 1991, the educational community continues to debate the issue with viewpoints being divided between those agreeing with Clark, those agreeing with Kozma, and those stuck somewhere between the two. Kozma contested Clark's conclusions by stating that "capabilities of a particular medium" in conjunction with teaching strategies, influence how learners process information in order to construct knowledge (Clark, 2012, p. 104). Kozma asserts that learning is an active and strategic process in which the learner combines information from his or her learning environment with prior knowledge. Komza defines learning as an "active, constructive, cognitive, and social process by which the learner strategically manages available cognitive, physical, and social resources to create new knowledge by interacting with information in the environment and integrating it with information stored in memory" (Kozma, p. 1). Kozma adds that cognitive factors such as long- and short-term memory structure and content control the learning process (Clark, 2012).

Kozma agrees with Clark's argument that some students will be able to learn regardless of the media; however, he feels that Clark's position must be modified (Clark, 2012, p. 137). Kozma further encourages more research on the way learners process information presented by different forms of media. Additionally,

TEACHTHOUGHT
4 STAGES: THE INTEGRATION OF TECHNOLOGY IN LEARNING

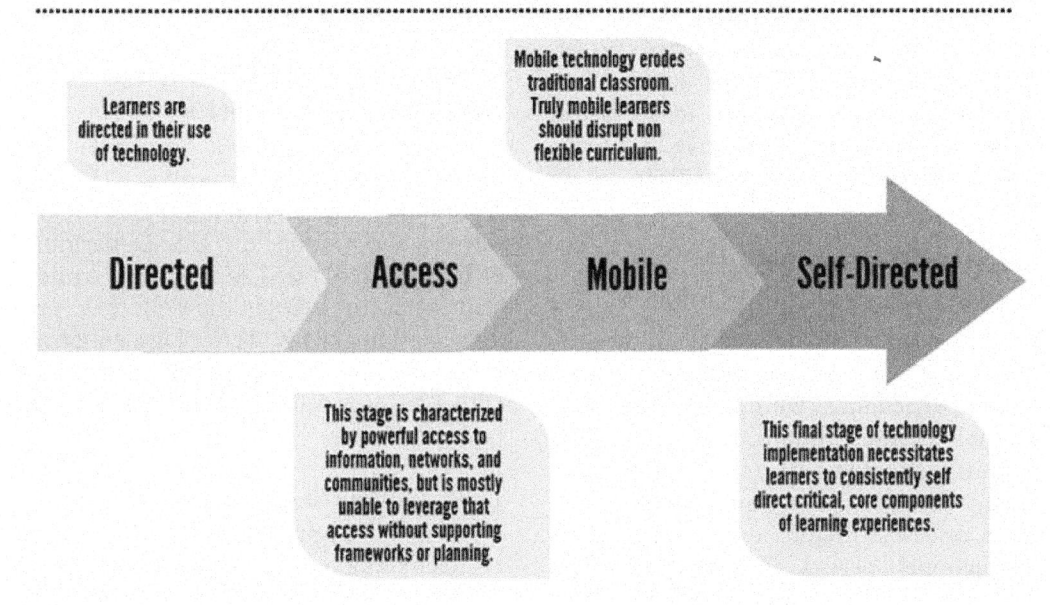

Directed — Learners are directed in their use of technology.

Access — This stage is characterized by powerful access to information, networks, and communities, but is mostly unable to leverage that access without supporting frameworks or planning.

Mobile — Mobile technology erodes traditional classroom. Truly mobile learners should disrupt non flexible curriculum.

Self-Directed — This final stage of technology implementation necessitates learners to consistently self direct critical, core components of learning experiences.

Figure 2. Demonstration of the flow to achieve effective technology integration.

Kozma points out that learner perceptions of a "particular medium and the purposes they have for viewing" can influence the amount of effort they put into the processing of the information (Clark, 2012, p. 118).

Kozma opposes Clark's stance that media and instructional strategies are separate components. He asserts that media and instructional strategies have an "integral relationship, as both are part of instructional design" (Clark, 2012, p. 138).

While there is evidence to support Clark's stance, the needs of 21st century learners, as addressed by Kozma, have caused educators to rethink instructional best practices.

21ST CENTURY LEARNERS' NEEDS

Classroom technology integration is more challenging than it was in the past due the increase of technology use for recreational purposes that has altered the "learning styles, strengths, and preferences" of 21st century students (Dede, 2007, p. 11). Additionally, according to Hodges and McTigue (2014), preparing middle school students for the demands of an evolving 21st century technology-driven world "while attending to adolescents' rapidly changing cognitive, psychological, and social needs presents teachers with an even more dynamic challenge" (p. 2). According to Lawrence and O'Brien (2012), a study of an urban middle school concluded that the No Child Left Behind (NCLB) Act caused a decline of instructional time in social studies and science content area courses, causing the use of digital tools to be more critical for middle school teachers. Middle school teachers must learn ways to effectively utilize online social media, such "blogs, wikis, RSS tagging and social bookmarking, music-photo-video sharing, mashups, podcasts, digital storytelling, virtual communities, social network services, virtual environments, and video blogs" (Rheingold, 2008, p. 100) Therefore, traditional approaches are less appealing to students (Chrisman & Harvey, 1998). Additionally, traditional approaches fail to adequately support students in acquiring the knowledge needed to strive in a technology-driven society (Shane, 2009).

What Is Technology Integration?

Before we can address the challenges associated with integrating technology into school curriculums, we must define what technology integration is. Hamilton (2007) defines technology integration as the use of any technology or device to support, teach, or assess student learning during an instructional period. Teachers must be skilled in technology integration by using it as a method of teaching, communication, and assessment (Howery, 2001). Overbaugh and Lu (2008) affirm that teachers must be able to use a wide array of technology to enhance their curriculum, if they are to be considered fully competent integrating technology.

Technology Integration Levels

According to Kim and Baylor (2008), despite the efforts of schools to provide teachers with computers, educational software, and technology training, many teachers do not effectively integrate technology into their curriculum. Many teachers have not progressed beyond using technology for their own productivity and creating teaching materials. The evaluation of the *Enhancing Education Through Technology Program: Final Report* noted that only 15 states indicated that they are meeting their state's definition of full technology integration (Bakia, Means, Gallagher, Chen, & Jones, 2009). Additionally, although there has been an increase in teacher use of technology to support teacher productivity, there was no evidence that the frequency of student technology use for learning increased.

Governmental Technology Integration Funding

The 2006 21st Century No Child Left Behind, Enhancing Education Through Technology Title II D (NCLB II-D) Year 3 Review, reports that the U.S. Department of Education allotted $700 million to help state school agencies in their efforts to provide students with technology-enhanced lessons (State Educational Technology Directors Association, 2006). The initiative had three goals

1. to improve student academic achievement through the use of technology in elementary and secondary schools;
2. to assist every student in crossing the digital divide by ensuring that every student is technology literate by the time the student finishes eighth grade, regardless of race, ethnicity, gender, family income, geographic location, and disability; and
3. to encourage the effective integration of technology resources and systems with teacher training and curriculum development to establish research-based instructional methods that can be widely implemented as best practices by state education agencies and local education agencies.

Although 14 states reported that prior to NCLB II-D funding their state did not have a source for funding technology, it is evident that funding is not the only factor that hinders a high level of technology integration. The report concluded that roughly 22% of state school agencies require that school improvement process include technology integration (State Edu-

Using Technology	Technology Integration
Technology usage is random, arbitrary & often an afterthought	Technology usage is planned & purposeful
Technology is rare or sporadically used in the classroom	Technology is a routine part of the classroom environment
Technology is used purely for the sake of using technology	Technology is used to support curricular goals & learning objectives
Technology is used to instruct students on content	Technology is used to engage students with content
Technology is mostly being used by the instructor(s)	Technology is mostly being used by the student(s)
Focus on simply using technologies	Focus on using technologies to create and develop new thinking processes
More instructional time is spent learning how to use the technology	More instructional time is spent using the technology to learn
Technology is used to complete lower-order thinking tasks	Technology is used to encourage higher-order thinking skills
Technology is used solely by individuals working alone	Technology is used to facilitate collaboration in & out of the classroom
Technology is used to facilitate activities that are feasible or easier without technology	Technology is used to facilitate activities that would otherwise be difficult or impossible
Technology is used to deliver information	Technology is used to construct & build knowledge
Technology is peripheral to the learning activity	Technology is essential to the learning activity

© TeachBytes 2013

Figure 3. Technology use verses technology integration.

cational Technology Directors Association, 2006).

The United States Department of Education established the Common Core State Standards in 2010 to establish consistent educational standards for all students across the country. The purpose was to help ensure that all U.S. students graduate from high school "college and career ready," possessing the skills to "earn a self-sustaining wage or participate in postsecondary education without remediation" (National Governors Association Center for Best Practices & Council of Chief State School Officers, 2010, p. 12). To achieve these skills, students need instruction and practice in "(a) using digital tools and online resources; (b) engaging in argument, reasoning, and problem solving; and (c) collaborating on authentic tasks that require academic reading, writing, and research" (National Governors Association Center for Best Practices & Council of Chief State School Officers, 2010, p. 12).

TECHNOLOGY INTEGRATION BARRIERS

Overbaugh and Lu (2008) assert that there is a strong relationship between teachers' educational beliefs and their instructional decisions and classroom practices. Teachers must consider technology to be personally meaningful before they can use it to enhance student learning. Additionally, teachers must believe that they can implement technology effectively, as well as possess the technological skills to do so. Without a sufficient level of self-efficacy for performing computer tasks, technology integration may not even be attempted (Oliver & Shapiro, 1993).

According to Bandura (1997) the first step toward developing the capacity to perform a particular skill is building self-efficacy. Self-efficacy is "a judgment of how well one can perform across a variety of situations" (Nel & Boshoff, 2016, p. 38). An individual's perceived level of self-efficacy influences his or her "motivational state as it involves the individual's beliefs regarding his or her abilities to perform and succeed at tasks" (Nel & Boshoff, 2016, p. 38). In regards to technology integration, self-efficacy refers to a teacher's persistence with which he/she will try to create technology enriched lessons (Overbaugh & Lu, 2008). Hall and Martin (2008) concluded from a pilot study that instructors with high levels of technology self-efficacy tend to demonstrate more perseverance and creative techniques to incorporate technology into their curriculum. Hall and Martin state that factors such as "grade level taught, the content area, the experience level of the teacher, and professional development" contribute to teachers' levels of self-efficacy in regards to technology integration (2009, p. 5).

Bull et al. (2008) emphasize that there are several issues that act as constraints to effective technology integration.

1. School content must address specific learning objectives.
2. Many learning objectives are subject to time constraints.
3. Addition of technology can increase the complexity of classroom management.
4. Schools are heavily invested in print technologies and often constrain Internet access in ways that limit access to online media tools.
5. Teachers have limited models for effective integration of media in their teaching.
6. Only limited research is available to guide best practice.

The authors add that these factors explain why the global spread of technology usage for recreational purposes outside school has yet to be employed with equal effectiveness inside schools.

INEFFECTIVE TRAINING

Research suggests the ill-preparedness of teachers is attributed to training that rarely goes beyond technical skills (Kim & Baylor, 2008), teacher training in the form of workshops (Gulamhussein, 2013) and lack of organizational support during the implementation phase of new technology (Ermeling, 2010). Gualamhussein's (2013) report asserts that staff development must move beyond the traditional practice of supplying teachers with knowledge as a means to train them to integrate technology. Teachers will need additional training to turn their newly acquired knowledge into effective practice. Erekson and Shumway (2006) concluded that many tradi-

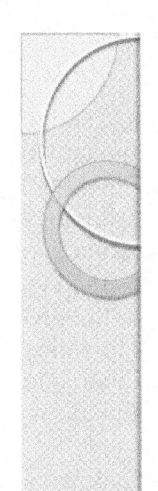

Universality

Students are diverse and global, by successfully integrating technology into classrooms we can prepare them for life and future careers

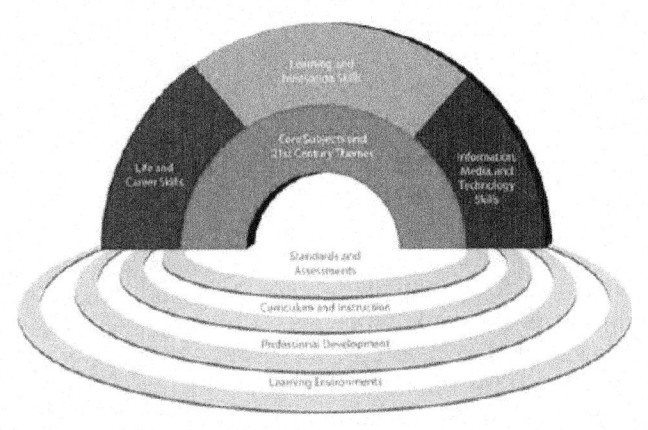

Figure 4. Twenty-first century learners need technology skills in order to compete in a technology-driven society.

tional classroom settings can remain very effective when combined with instructional technology.

As technology becomes more commonplace in classrooms, teachers should focus the use of technology to help 21st century students gain the knowledge and skills required to compete in technology-driven society (Kelley, 2013). Means (2010) concluded through research that effective training is directly related to the content area that the instructor teaches, delivered through multiple sessions over time, consists of follow-up activities, and engages participants at their current knowledge and skill levels. Additionally, evidence suggests that teachers consider professional development to be more beneficial when they participate with other teachers from their work environment, because they have a support group that allows them to complete their professional development goals (Means, 2010). Studies show that teachers view technology professional development as useful mainly when it is related to their area of specialization and content taught.

Teachers are often not provided with effective technology integration models; and there is "limited research available to guide best practice" (Bull et al., 2008, p. 102). Teachers need teaching models that enable them to conceptualize how to use various programs to enhance teaching and learning. Effective modeling includes student technology use, technology utilized in small and large group instruction, and content specific technology utilization. Additionally, teachers need opportunities to collaborate with other teachers using the same technology.

Research also suggests that school climate and support should be changed to foster effective technology integration. The climate for technology integration should allow for experimentation to help eliminate the fear of failure (Overbaugh & Lu, 2008). Support for technology integration is one of the areas that is often neglected by schools' technology training personnel. Technology support should be on-site, ongoing, expeditious to be effective.

Lee (2006) offers strategies for school administrators that can be used to support teachers in their efforts to integrate technology.

- plan professional development that provides a vision of how integrated technology can look in the classroom;
- model ways that technology can be used to support standards-based curriculum;
- create opportunities for teachers to share about how they use computers within schools and between schools;
- offer more training on how to integrate technology into curriculum;
- offer training on how to use computers to teach content in instructional areas, rather than how to use specific software programs;
- consider creative ways to increase the number of teachers who attend technology training sessions;
- for teachers who are hesitant to integrate technology, provide more training on classroom management and hot maximize the amount of computer time available; and
- incorporate funds for updating hardware and software in technology budgets any time new technology is acquired.

BENEFITS OF EFFECTIVE TRAINING

Teachers who frequently integrate technology understand the value of technology to students' academic careers. Lee (2006) asserts that teachers that value technology understand that technology experience is necessary for students' future success, technology further enables them to meet students' various needs by addressing their learning styles and preferences, and technology can enhance the quality of student work.

In addition to preparing 21st century students to thrive in a technology-driven society, technology integration offers benefits. Teachers that are effectively integrating technology are more likely to cultivate classroom management practices that maximize technology usage time for students, use computers as a tool to produce quality student work, attend more technology training, take the initiative to develop technology activities for students, ask for help with integration issues, and share technology ideas with other teachers (Lee, 2006).

In a study of teachers who are considered to be expert technology users by their peers, Becker (2006) concluded that expert technology users "directly address curriculum goals by having students use a variety of computer software, including simulations, programming languages, spreadsheets, database programs, graphing programs, logic and problem-solving programs, writing tools, and electronic bulletin-board communications software" (p. 274).

The presence of certain characteristics increases the probability to develop into an exemplary technology innovator. The characteristics are:

- working in an environment with several other technology users;
- computer use for consequential activities such as writing and simulations;

- access to an on-site technology coordinator for support; and
- working in a resource-rich environment.

TEACHERS AS DECISION MAKERS

In addition to improving technology training practices, providing support throughout the implementation phase, and creating a climate that encourages and rewards technology integration, school administrators can further increase technology integrations levels by including teachers in the technology decision-making process. Hamilton (2007) concludes that schools with high technology integration levels have an on-site, teacher-only technology committee. In addition to decision-making power, those committees are "empowered with a budget" (p. 28). Teachers in those environments are motivated to increase their use of technology because they feel included in the decision-making process, therefore feeling that their needs and wants were considered. In order for an innovation to be adopted by a social system, Rogers (1995) noted that it must be perceived to be advantageous and be compatible to current values. Teacher-only committees are "able to influence other individuals' attitudes or overt behavior informally in a desired way with relative frequency" (p. 27). Peer opinion plays a large part in influencing decisions. Rogers states that individuals will value the opinions of their peers more than scientific research and decisions "made by relatively a few individuals in a system who possess power, status, or technical expertise" (p. 38).

CONCLUSION

It is evident that more research is needed to discover best practices for technology integration. However, current research suggests guidelines that administrators can follow to support effective technology integration in their schools. By following the guidelines mentioned above school administrators will be able to effectively support teachers in their technology integration efforts. A supportive environment will give teachers the confidence they need to effectively design technology enhanced instruction that "more directly and powerfully" influences student learning outcomes (Clark, 2012).

REFERENCES

Aslan, S. (2015). Is learning by teaching effective in gaining 21st century skills? The views of pre-service science teachers. *Educational Sciences, 15(6),* 1441–1457. doi:10.12738/estp.2016.1.019

Bakia, M., Means, B., Gallagher, L., Chen, E., & Jones, K. (2009). *Evaluation of the enhancing education through technology program: Final report.* Retrieved from https://www2.ed.gov/rschstat/eval/tech/netts/finalreport.pdf

Bandura, A. (1997). *Self-efficacy: The exercise of control.* New York, NY: W.H. Freeman.

Becker, H. J. (2000). How exemplary computer-using teachers differ from other teachers: Implications for realizing the potential of computers in schools. *Contemporary Issues in Technology and Teacher Education, 1*(2), 274–293.

Bull, G., Thompson, A., Searson, M., Garofalo, J., Park, J., Young, C., & Lee, J. (2008). Connecting informal and formal learning: Experiences in the age of participatory media. *Contemporary Issues in Technology and Teacher Education, 8*(2), 100–107.

Chrisman, N. R., & Harvey, F. (1998). Extending the classroom: Hypermedia-supported learning. *Journal of Geography in Higher Education, 22*(1), 11–18.

Clark, R. (2012). *Learning from media: Arguments, analysis, and evidence.* Charlotte, NC, Information Age.

Dede, C. (2007). *Reinventing the role of information and communications technologies in education.* In L. Smolin, K. Lawless, & N. C. Burbules (Eds.), *Information and communication technologies: Considerations of current practice for teachers and teacher educators* (pp. 11–38). Malden, MA: Blackwell

Ermeling, B. (2009). Tracing the effects of teacher inquiry on classroom practice. *Teaching and Teacher Education, 26*(3), 377–388.

Erekson, T., & Shumway, S. (2006). Integrating the study of technology into the curriculum: A consulting teacher model. *Journal of Technology Education, 18*(1) 27–28.

Gulamhussein, A. (2013). *Teaching the teachers effective staff development in an era of high stakes accountability*. Retrieved from Center for Public Schools website: http://www.centerforpubliceducation.org/Main-Menu/Staffingstudents/Teaching-the-Teachers-Effective-Professional-Development-in-an-Era-of-High-Stakes-Accountability/Teaching-the-Teachers-Full-Report.pdf

Hamilton, B. (2007). It's elementary! Technology integration in the primary grades. Retrieved from the International Society for Technology Education website: http://www.iste.org/images/excerpts/ITSELE-excerpt.pdf

Hall, B., & Martin, K. (2009, June). *Relationships among computer self-efficacy, professional development, teaching experience and technology instruction for teachers.* Presented at the National Educational Computing Conference, Washington, DC.

Hodges, T., & McTigue, E. (2014). Renovating literacy centers for middle grades: Differentiating, reteaching, and motivating. *The Clearing House, 87*(4), 155–160.

Howery, P. (2001). *Teacher technology training: A study of the impact of educational technology on teacher attitude and student achievement* (Doctoral dissertation). La Sierra University, Riverside, CA.

Kelley, T. R. (2013). STL guiding the 21st century thinker. *Technology & Engineering Teacher, 73*(4), 18–23.

Kim, C., & Baylor, A. L. (2008). A virtual change agent: Motivating pre-service teachers to integrate technology in their future classrooms. *Journal of Educational Technology & Society, 11*(2), 309–321.

Kimble, C. (1999). The impact of technology on learning: Making sense of the research (Policy Brief). *Mid-Continent Regional Educational Lab, 7*, 2–8.

Kozma, R. (1994). The influence of media on learning: The debate continues. *SLMQ, 22*(4), 1–13. Retrieved from http://www.ala.org/aasl/sites/ala.org.aasl/files/content/aaslpubsandjournals/slr/edchoice/SLMQ_InfluenceofMediaonLearning_InfoPower.pdf

Lawrence, N., & O'Brien, J. (2012). Using online collaborative tools to foster middle school students' "public voices": Payoffs, perils and possibilities. In I. Chen & D. McPheeters (Eds.) *Cases on educational technology integration in urban schools* (pp. 97–126). Hershey, PA: IGI Global. doi:10.4018/978-1-61350-492-5.ch023

Lee, W. (2006). *The relationship between teachers' beliefs and perceptions about student use of computers and how they integrate technology into curricular instruction* (Doctoral dissertation). University of California at Los Angeles.

Means, B. (2010). Technology and education change: Focus on student learning. *Journal of Research of Technology in Educations, 42*(3), 285–307.

National Governors Association Center for Best Practices & Council of Chief State School Officers. (2010). *Common core state standards for English language arts and literacy in history/social studies, science, and technical subjects*. Washington, DC: National Governors Association.

Nel, P., & Boshoff, A. (2016). Evaluating the factor structure of the general self-efficacy scale. *South African Journal of Psychology, 46*(1), 37–49. doi:10.1177/0081246315593070

Olivier, T. A., & Shapiro, F. (1993). Self-efficacy and computers. *Journal of Computer-Based Instruction, 20*(3), 81–85.

Overbaugh, R., & Lu, R. (2008). The impact of a NCLB-EETT funded professional development program on teacher self-efficacy and resultant implementation. *Journal of Research on Technology in Education, 41*(1), 43–61.

Partnership for 21st Century Skills. (2008). *21st century skills, education, and competitiveness*. Washington, DC: Author.

Rheingold, H. (2008). Using participatory media and public voice to encourage civic engagement. In W. L. Bennett (Ed.), *Civic life online: Learning how digital media can engage youth* (pp. 97–118). Cambridge, MA: The MIT Press.

Rogers, E. M. (1995). *Diffusion of innovations* (4th ed.). New York, NY: The Free Press.

Shana, Z. (2009). Learning with technology: Using discussion forums to augment a traditional-style class. *Journal of Educational Technology & Society, 12*(3), 214–228.

State Educational Technology Directors Association. (2006). *National trends: Enhancing education through technology No Child Left Behind, Title II D* (Rep.). (2006, March). Retrieved from State Educational Technology Directors Association website: http://files.eric.ed.gov/fulltext/ED537537.pdf

Edited by Anymir Orellana, Terry L. Hudgins, & Michael Simonson

The Perfect Online Course

BEST PRACTICES FOR DESIGNING AND TEACHING

A Volume in
Perspectives in Instructional Technology
and Distance Education

Get Your Copy Today—Information Age Publishing

The Major Role of Financial Aid Guidance During the Enrollment Process

Richard Hudnett

Among the many responsibilities that a university's financial aid department might have is educating students about their options for paying tuition. In a study conducted by the researcher that aimed to learn more about why an admitted student decides not to enroll, five of the six participants expressed issues with some aspect of the university's financial aid process, and four of the six participants cited some level of financial aid dissatisfaction during their experience within the university's admission process.

Richard Hudnett,
4850 Millenia Blvd., Orlando, FL 32839.
Telephone: (407) 494-1014.
E-mail: hudnett@nova.edu

One of the three major themes revealed during the researchers study was the important role of financial aid guidance during the enrollment process. Three current trends that potentially indicate the number of prospective students relying on a university's financial aid guidance with their academic tuition and costs will rise in the future include the following (a) the increasing cost of a college education within the United States, (b) the rise in postsecondary enrollment rates, and (c) the increasing demand for financial aid by postsecondary undergraduates. According to the National Center for Education Statistics (2015a), the cost of a college education rose 25% at private, nonprofit institutions between 2003–2004 and 2013–2014. Furthermore, student enrollment at degree-granting postsecondary institutions increased 20% between these years as well (2015b). Not only did both of these indicators rise, but also the percentage of first-time degree/certificate seeking undergraduates at 4-year institutions requesting financial aid. The National Center for Education Statistics (2015c) noted this figure increased 5% between the academic years of 2008–8 and 2012–2013.

Two of the primary sources of a prospective student's financial aid information should be from the office of Federal Student Aid and the financial aid department at the university they are interested in attending. Both of these financial aid resources, one directly managed by the federal government and the other by university personnel, can have a significant impact on a prospective student's enrollment experience. Both entities are the two most trusted and reliable sources for a student's financial aid services. The role of a university's financial aid services will not only increase due to the trends reflecting possible increases in the needs of prospective students, but it will also expand its already significant role in helping educate and provide prospective students with accurate and timely financial aid assistance.

Regardless of whether or not prospective students believe they qualify for financial aid, they should still consider completing a Free Application for Student Financial Aid (FASFA) because it may be an existing eligibility requirement for certain scholarships at various schools (FASFA, 2016). Moreover, the reason why prospective students decide not to complete their FASFA can simply be irrelevant or inaccurate. The FASFA (2016) website highlights several of the most common misconceptions by prospective students about its eligibility requirements, which include the following: (a) the applicant's age (b) the applicant's family income, and (c) the applicant's prior academic success or grade point average. It is essential for prospective students to rely on factual information regarding their financial aid eligibility because it can alter their academic path tremendously. For example, if prospective students believe they are ineligible for financial aid assistance, it can likely influence important decisions such as (a) what college they decide to apply to or attend, (b) how many classes they enroll in, (c) which semester they begin enrollment, and (d) what certificate or degree they can afford to pursue. Therefore, it can be extremely valuable for prospective students to be aware of legitimate FASFA eligibility requirements in order to reduce the likelihood of making a poor decision that alters their academic path and is based on false information.

The FASFA website not only provides prospective students with accurate eligibility requirements and the ability to submit their application online, it also offers the opportunity to learn a great deal more about the college search process, key financial definitions, college cost comparison guides, and much more college-related preparatory information. Available advice that can be found on the FASFA website ranges from how an elementary student can begin preparing for college to a university's scorecard, which compares current information about a college's graduation rates, annual estimated tuition, and average earnings of its graduates. The FASFA website should be among a prospective student's most reliable and trustworthy sources because it is an office of the U.S. Department of Education and the provider of over $150 billion in federal aid to students.

Although the FASFA website should be among a prospective student's primary sources of financial aid information, it encourages its website visitors to learn more about the financial aid process by contacting the financial aid office at the schools they are interested in attending. Moreover, there are many prospective students who begin the process of financially planning to attend college by either reviewing literature provided to them by a college or through some other form of communication with a college's financial aid office. Therefore, prospective students are not only encouraged to trust, but also to rely on a university's financial aid office for financial aid guidance and pertinent FASFA-related information such as key application deadline dates.

Universities that are interested in exploring why an admitted student fails to enroll might likely want to consider measuring a prospective student's level of satisfaction within key enrollment stages, such a student's experience with its financial aid office. In a recent study conducted by the writer exploring why an admitted student failed to enroll, several of the participants did in fact discuss their experience within a university's financial aid office and, for some of the study's participants, their experiences did influence their decision not to enroll.

Five of the six participants in the researcher's study expressed issues with some aspect of the university's financial aid process. Specifically, two of the participants attributed their failure to enroll to a financial aid "roadblock" they experienced or the "lack of financial aid information" (Hudnett, 2015). When Participant 1 was asked to describe what led her to never enroll at the university, she stated that the "financial part was the main reason." Although the first participant also found the university's tuition to be "too expensive," she also stated that "financial aid could have helped me create a better road map to pay for the degree," and "I would have liked to have gotten assigned to a financial aid person to help me with this." The second participant stated during her interview that she "was a bit confused about how to figure out the financial aid process." The third participant referenced several issues addressing the topic of financial aid with the university that included a few of the following statements: (a) the "financial aid side was confusing"; (b) "financial aid was a roadblock"; (c) it was a "headache trying to figure out how to pay for classes"; and (d) "I got fed up with trying to figure the financial aid process." The fourth participant had no issue with the financial aid process; however, it was never successfully communicated to her that she was admitted to the university. The fifth participant stated that she encountered a "halt in her financial aid process and many questions never got answered." Moreover, when the fifth participant was asked what were some of her unanswered enrollment questions before or after she submitted her application, she stated that, "I needed to know more about my financial aid hold." The final participant, Participant 6, did in fact enroll, but quickly dropped her course and was billed for the class, which she did not complete. She is still disputing the charges. Furthermore, when asked to describe her reason for not enrolling, in her case re-enrolling for her first class that she did not complete, she stated that it's due to the lack of financial aid "available funds" (Hudnett, 2015).

Four of the participants cited some level of financial aid dissatisfaction during their experience in the university's admission process in addition to further describing this as one of the primary reasons why they never enrolled. A university's financial aid department can have many responsibilities; however, among the most important is providing current and prospective students with accurate financial aid information. One of the emerging themes that resulted from a recent study by Ziskin, Fischer, Torres, Pellicciotti, and Player-Sanders (2014), which focused on the perception college students have on how they will pay for their college tuition, was that the majority of its participants felt anxious and uncertain about their entire financial aid process. Moreover, the students' negative feelings were primarily due to lack of clarity and information about the university's financial aid processes. Similar to Ziskin et al.'s findings, many of the participants in this study expressed the need for more complete and accurate financial aid information and guidance (Hudnett, 2015).

The second participant, who eventually enrolled at the university, attributes doing so to eventually getting the answers to her outstanding questions, several on the topic of her financial aid. The fourth participant, one of the two participants who enrolled at a different university, never knew she was admitted and, therefore, did not have any difficulty with the financial aid process. The importance for financial aid is a combination of the first interpretation that a need exists for a personalized experience, relevant to a student's financial aid. The second interpretation is that a breakdown in communication occurred at some point between the participant and the university's financial aid process, which led to a failure to enroll (Hudnett, 2015).

Prospective students, along with many other students, who are anticipating the use of federal loans to pay for their college tuition expenses will very likely receive information or establish some level of communication with a university's financial aid office. The success of a university's communication with its prospective admitted students relative to each of their personal financial aid needs can likely determine if they in fact enroll. The research findings revealed in this study indicated that the majority of the study's participants who failed to enroll expressed issues with some aspect of the university's financial aid process and cited some level of financial aid dissatisfaction during the process.

REFERENCES

Free Application for Federal Student Aid. (2016). Federal student aid. Retrieved from https://fafsa.ed.gov/

Hudnett, R. (2015). Understanding the admissions experience of admitted students who fail to enroll: A multiple case study (Doctoral dissertation). Retrieved from http://nsuworks.nova.edu/cgi/viewcontent.cgi?article=1019&context=fse_etd

National Center for Education Statistics. (2015a). Fast facts: Tuition costs of colleges and universities. Retrieved from https://nces.ed.gov/fastfacts/display.asp?id=76

National Center for Education Statistics. (2015b). Fast facts: Enrollment. Retrieved from https://nces.ed.gov/fastfacts/display.asp?id=98

National Center for Education Statistics. (2015c). Fast facts: Financial aid. Retrieved from https://nces.ed.gov/FastFacts/display.asp?id=31

Ziskin, M., Fischer, M. A., Torres, V., Pellicciotti, B., & Player-Sanders, J. (2014). Working students' perceptions of paying for college: Understanding the connections between financial aid and work. *Review of Higher Education, 37*(4), 429–467.

A Brief History of E-Learning in Post-Soviet Armenia

Varvara Gasparyan

INTRODUCTION

Since the early 1970s, distance education has gained unprecedented popularity, grounded in a system of science, methods, and technology (Moore & Kearsley, 2012). It became the most dramatic of the technology-based innovations influencing education (Simonson, Smaldino, Albright, & Zvacek, 2012). One form of distance education, electronic learning or "e-learning," is widespread, developing as a new learning environment using Internet technologies and multimedia applications. With the advancement of the technology, the electronic environment enables learning activities in a convenient way with access to information in time and space independently.

The source of the term *e-learning* is uncertain; however, it has been suggested that it originated in the 1980s about the same time that the term *online learning* was coined (Moore, Dickson-Deane, & Galyen, 2010). According to Hall (as cited in Orellana, Hudgins, & Simonson, 2009), e-learning is the acquisition of knowledge and skills through a variety of technological means. The National Center for Supercomputing Applications (2000) adopted as its the definition of e-learning, "the acquisition and use of knowledge distributed and facilitated primarily by electronic means." Saba (2011) reported that e-learning is an inadequate concept for building a comprehensive theory of distance education and e-learning courses cannot be presented as fully implemented distance education programs. Simonson et al. (2012) stated that "distance education should not be confused with e-learning, which is considered an outdated term" (p. 83). However, with all this explanation of e-learning, it should be noted that all definitions of e-learning are differentiated by applications, programs, or websites as forms of e-learning that afford a learning opportunity to learners.

Varvara Gasparyan,
12 Fortini St Apt. 1R, Cranston, RI 02920.
Telephone: (401) 946-9196.
E-mail: varvaravan@yahoo.com

In post-Soviet countries, the terms *e-learning* and *distance education* were confused (Zawacki-Richter & Kourotchkina, 2012). In post-Soviet Armenia, the concept of e-learning follows the perception of online learning and distance learning. The purpose of this article is to briefly explore the adoption of e-learning activities implemented in the Armenia over a period of more than a decade that have become popular among many of its citizens. To understand e-learning activities in Armenia, it is necessary to explain the transformations of the country's educational policies and processes, which are closely related to the political system. The history of education may be divided into two stages: the Soviet period and the post-Soviet period. E-learning as a form of teaching and learning was established in Armenia after separation from the Soviet regime. Armenia became an independent state and, in the post-Soviet period, transitioned with the educational modifications.

In Armenia, with a history of literacy going back 1,600 years, education has always received priority and is a central factor for maintaining national identity and heritage (Melik-Baxshian, 2012). Armenia was incorporated into the Soviet Union in 1922. During nearly 70 years under the Soviet regime, the country has enhanced its educational system beginning with population illiteracy elimination, establishing a 10-year public school system, 2-year education colleges, and advancing universities in the country's capital and in remote cities. Armenia advanced its educational priorities and enabled the population to become higher educational professionals and scientists in a variety of spheres. In 1960, Armenia had a literacy rate of 100% (Curtis, 1995).

EDUCATIONAL CHALLENGES

EDUCATIONAL REFORMS IN ARMENIA

After the Soviet Union's collapse in 1990, Armenia declared its independence, and, according to the Armenian Declaration of Independence (1990), "the Republic creates its own system of education and of scientific and cultural development" (Article 10). Armenia's citizens declared its sovereignty and its country as an independent and democratic state. As a first priority, Armenia began making modifications in the inherited Soviet educational system.

In the years after gaining independence, the people of Armenia experienced a painful transition process from a centralized planned economy to the free market, ethnic conflicts, a war with Azerbaijan for the Armenian enclave Nagorno-Karabakh, economic crisis and economic blockade, broken energy resources, and industrial life. All these reasons were multifold in cutting state financing (Melikyan, 2004). The routine lives of the citizens were completely disrupted and the state did not have any allocations for education, which had a catastrophic impact on the education system of Armenia. There was a need to implement tremendous changes in all spheres of life in the country. It started with educational changes and reforms. On December 14, 2004, Armenia adopted *The Law on Higher Education and Postgraduate Professional Education.* The basic principles of the law were to regulate legal, organizational, and financial relations in the sphere of higher and postgraduate education in the country (Armenian National Information Center for Academic Recognition and Mobility, 2005).

Armenia is located in Eastern Europe and its citizens wanted to become a part of European higher education. Because the structure of Soviet-type education was different and incompatible with the European educational standards, Armenia's educational leaders were interested in making the country's academic degrees and education quality assurance standards compatible with the higher education system of other European countries. Armenia signed an agreement with the European Union to become a part of the

European Neighborhood. However, though Armenia became a part of the European area, its incompatibility in some spheres of society relations prevented the building of full relations with the western countries. In 1999, European education ministers from 28 countries gathered at the University of Bologna and signed the Declaration of Bologna (The Bologna Declaration, 1999), thereby agreeing that the European Higher Education Area countries had to adopt a system of comparable and compatible degrees, the education system had to be based on two main cycles, a credit system in education had to be established, focus was on lifelong learning, and adaptation of doctoral degree studies and synergy between the European Higher Education Area and European Research Area. This agreement was based on a stringent set of guidelines. Biannual ministerial meetings were arranged so the members could check on the condition of work completed and set guidelines for upcoming years. A framework of three cycles of higher education qualifications was adopted: bachelor's degree, master's degree, and doctoral degree.

In 2005, Armenia joined the European Agreement of Higher Education, which was called the Bologna Process (Bologna Process, 2005). The goal of the Bologna Process was to provide responses to the issues of the public responsibility for higher education and research, higher education governance, and roles for individuals in higher education and research with the demanding qualification needs (The Bologna Declaration, 1999). By 2010, Armenia had to develop its national qualifications framework and to combine it into one efficient system compatible with the main framework of Europe, according to the European standards (The Framework of Qualifications for the European Higher Education Area, 2005).

Armenia made overall changes and reforms in its post-Soviet transition period, which included the extension of school years, changes to the grading system, and creation of separate high schools. The country started transitioning its 10-year schooling system to a 12-year education cycle, by changing to 11 years in 2001 and to 12 years in 2006, where primary, intermediate, and high schools were created. Changes to the grading system consisted of shifting 5-point grading to a 10-point grading system, and helped to ensure pupils' assessment results were more accurate. They became effective in September 2012.

The meticulous information on the educational reforms confirmed the large and beneficial transformation made in the post-Soviet transitional period. Due to this transformation, Armenia was invited to become a participant of the European educational programs, such as *Tempus* and *Erasmus Mundus* among others (National Tempus Offices, 2014). Participation in those programs gave the Armenian specialists an opportunity to gain experience in the European quality assurance system, and to be involved in the students' exchange and training programs. Based on these programs, training, as well as e-learning and distance learning programs were implemented.

BEGINNING OF E-LEARNING IN ARMENIA

Beginning in 2004, with the partnership and collaboration of the European Union countries and the U.S. educational institutions—the Open University in United Kingdom, the University of Connecticut School of Social Work in the United States, the International Institute of Sociology in Sweden, and the Irish Association of Social Workers in the Republic of Ireland, Armenia was able to establish the Distance Learning Laboratory at the Yerevan State University. This laboratory was created in the framework of the Tempus Joint European Project. Simultaneously, branches of the Distance Learning Laboratory were organized at regional centers in Gyumri, Vanadzor, and Ijevan. The mission of the distance learning centers is to provide the population with accessible and affordable education and training prospects (Mkrtichyan, 2007). The faculty at the Distance Learning Laboratory provides 1-year distance learning programs in a range of subjects: social work, social pedagogy, public relations and marketing, human resources, sales and services, sociology, psychology, philosophy, economics, international relations, Armenian studies, and English language. The programs are taught in the Armenian and English languages (Distance Learning Beyond Any Limit, 2016).

At the Yerevan State University (2007) with the help of New York University and the U.S. Agency for International Development, assistance was established for the next learning center, including distance education—the Information Technologies Educational and Research Centre. The center serves as a hub for educational programs with traditional education, online distance education, and scientific research. Staff at the Information Technologies Educational and Research Centre is involved in the implementation of education e-governmental and quality assurance systems.

In the last decade, Armenia has witnessed rapid growth of online activities through varied learning programs; online learning was becoming an increasing part of the education sphere. Armenians became more interested, they were able to purchase technological equipment and establish an Internet connection, and distance learning has become more positively regarded. Traditional universities and colleges began to offer online courses in a variety of subjects, such as business, education, Armenian and foreign languages, history, art, and psychology.

With the collaboration of the European Union Tacis Project in Armenia in the period of 1999–2000, a project was developed to enhance skills in business, government, agriculture, and civil society (Commission of the European Communities, 2000; Tacis Project in Armenia, 2000). In the background of the Tacis project, a distance education pilot project course was implemented in preparation for the Association of Accountants and Auditors of Armenia. The course was organized as the basis for the Armenian Legal Framework for Accounting, and simultaneously created the newly formed Association of Accountants and Auditors of Armenia. The entire package of this accountancy training program was covered by learning materials designed in accordance with the International Standards for Distance Education (Commission of the European Communities, 2000; Tacis Project in Armenia, 2000).

The Armenian Distance Learning Network was one of the first Armenian e-learning projects, which was created in 2002 and updated in 2006. This network e-learning project had a focus on the business of involving Armenian-speaking learners and developing e-business in the country. The first course was Electronic Commerce and used a book, *E-Commerce*, written specifically for it. The course was launched in 2004 with 50 e-learning participants. The second course had an enrolment of 150 participants and was welcomed by interested e-commerce learners.

One of the oldest and largest Armenian organizations, the Armenian Benevolent Union, was established in 1906 and actively operated in 28 countries. Its members have organized diverse educational programs in Armenia through the Armenian Virtual College. The Armenian Virtual College was launched in 2009 and is the country's first online Armenian college providing e-learning courses in Armenian and five other languages of instruction. Staff at the Armenian Virtual College have implemented teaching courses of Armenian culture and history by focusing on architecture, geography, fine arts, and music, as well as a chess program. They are unique programs enabling any learner to take online classes by choosing the language of instruction according to the language of choice (Western Armenian, Arabic, English, French, Spanish, and Russian). Students from various countries can participate in online courses. Teaching programs of the Armenian Virtual College are based on using the basic principles of the e-learning process (McLaren, 2009). College programs are implementing verbal, written, or graphic forms of teaching that make information interesting, vivid, and attractive, thereby avoiding the learning process passively conveying information. The learning theory is intended to allow the learners to store and retrieve that information easily, when needed, from working memory. The Armenian Virtual College (2016) includes an introduction for students with an interactive multimedia e-book series, presented by images and videos on different themes of Armenia's history, culture, economy, and more.

The Russian-Armenian (Slavonic) University, established in 1999, is in the joint authority of the Russian Federation and Republic of Armenia. It also collaborated in the European Commission Tempus Project with the involvement of universities in three countries of the South Caucasus: Armenian, Georgia, and Azerbaijan. The project included in its master's program in migration studies the establishment of the National Migration Competence Centers in each country. In Armenia, the framework of the Distance Learning Center was organized for 20 online learning courses covering a wide variety of programs by offering foreign languages, management, law, economics, information systems and design, among others (Russian-Armenian [Slavonic] University, 2016).

In Armenia, some centers of training and consulting services were organized in collaboration with the U.S. Agency for International Development through the Armenian private sector. The centers have online training courses and assessment and consulting services for the various spheres of the Armenian economy's private businesses to assist in organizing professional and quality assurance services for successful businesses.

The portal of the E-Learning Centre was established to support and develop e-learning programs at the Armenian educational institutions, and to enhance the quality of educational and scientific activities of distance learners and teachers. The list of online courses of this portal includes history of education, education, and computer learning (E-Learning Center, 2016).

The Enterprise Incubator Foundation (2014b), which was established in 2002, is a business and consulting services company that is supporting the development of the information and communication technology sector in Armenia. It is operated as a consulting service for business development and advisory services for country's instructional technology companies. Professionals of the company have organized online learning of Java, web, network foundations, and software programming for beginners in different regions of Armenia. The Enterprise Incubator Foundation (2014a) cooperates with Microsoft Corporation, Sun Microsystems, Cisco Systems, Hewlett Packard, Intel, and many other technological companies.

In 2009, Union of Armenian Medicine Producers and Importers, with the collaboration of the U.S. Agency for International Development, established the GXP Centre for Excellence. The GXP Centre for Excellence is a company involved in the area of manufacturing and distributing Armenian pharmaceutical and biotechnology production. It offers distance learning courses on professional topics developed by the international professionals in the pharmaceutical industry that have been approved by the Armenian Ministry of Health. In distance learning training courses, the staff at the center utilize a variety of types of instructional and educational technology with the cooperation of Armenian and international experts for its programs (GXP Centre for Excellence, 2014). The implementation of e-learning courses was organized as online courses in the state-owned and private educational institutions and learning centers with a mission to improve and develop the basic knowledge of the Armenian business and economy.

SUMMARY

E-learning was established and developed in Armenia in various ways. Some were organized on the basis of cooperation with the international higher institutions of the European Union countries by opening distance learning centers and offices at the universities or other higher education institutions in Armenia. Some were developed with the help of the U.S. Agency of International Development or the World Bank Services. Because the Armenian government is not able to finance all the organized e-learning centers and courses, most projects were based on European financial grants programs given to Armenia. Studies at the establishments of E-Laboratories and Centers included confirmation that not all classes are based on the seven principles for good practice in education. Seven general principles that are essential components for effective learning follow: (a) encourage student-faculty contact, (b) encourage cooperation among students, (c) encourage active learning, (d) give prompt feedback, (e) emphasize time on task, (f) communicate high expectations, and (g) respect diverse talent and ways of learning. To organize e-learning courses according to the seven principles of good practice, there is a need for good research on how to design those courses that will keep the learners active, because the active learning incorporates past experiences and allows students to talk and write about what they are learning (Sorensen & Baylen, 2009). Though all the points of seven principles of good practice were created for the traditional classroom instructions rather than the web environment, they can be used in the online environment by developing new strategies.

REFERENCES

Armenian Declaration of Independence. (1990). Retrieved from http://www.parliament.am/legislation.php?sel=show&ID=2602&lang=eng

Armenian National Information Center for Academic Recognition and Mobility. (2005). *The law of the Republic of Armenia on higher and postgraduate professional education*. Retrieved from http://www.armenic.am/

Armenian Virtual College. (2016). Armenian General Benevolent Union. Retrieved from http://agbu.org/education/armenian-virtual-college/

The Bologna Declaration. (1999). Retrieved from http://www.ehea.info/

Bologna Process. (2005). Communiqué of the Conference of European Ministers Responsible for Higher Education. Retrieved from http://www.armenic.am/?laid=1&

Commission of the European Communities. (2000, December 20). Report from the Commission: The TACIS Programmes Annual Report 1999. Tacis Project in Armenia. Retrieved from http://aei.pitt.edu/48192/1/COM_(1999)_835_final.pdf

Curtis, G. E. (Ed.). (1995). *Armenia: A country study*. Washington, DC: Government Printing Office.

Distance Learning Beyond Any Limit. (2016). Distance learning. Retrieved from http://www.distancelearning.am/index.php/en/

E-Learning Center. (2016). About the Portal E-learning Center (ELC). Retrieved from www.elearning.am

Enterprise Incubator Foundation. (2014a, June 2). Is e-learning becoming a reality in Armenia? 2013 state report. Retrieved from http://www.eif.am/eng/news/is-e-learning-becoming-a-reality-in-armenia/

Enterprise Incubator Foundation. (2014b). Project Enterprise Foundation. Retrieved from http://www.eif.am/eng/projects/

The Framework of Qualifications for the European Higher Education Area. (2005). Retrieved from http://www.ehea.info/uploads/qf/050520_framework_qualifications.pdf

GXP Centre for Excellence. (2014). Welcome to the official website of the GXP Centre for Excellence. Retrieved from http://www.gxp.am

McLaren, A. (2009). Designing effective e-learning. In A. Orellana, T. L. Hudgins, & M. Simonson (Eds.), *The perfect online course: Best practices for designing and teaching* (pp. 229–245). Charlotte, NC: Information Age.

Melik-Baxshian, M. (2012). Education in Armenia. Retrieved from http://www.ibe.unesco.org/curriculum/SoCaucasuspdf/Education%20in%20Armenia.pdf

Melikyan, H. (2004). Education reforms in the Republic of Armenia and the Bologna Process: Brief overview. Retrieved from http://www.erasmusmundus5.gr/scientific/Education_Reforms_in_the_RA_and_the_Bologna_Process

Mkrtichyan, A. E. (2007). Armenian statehood and the problems of European integration as reflected in school education. In T. Darieva & W. Kaschuba (Eds.), *Representations of the margins of Europe* (pp. 190–204). New York, NY: Campus. Retrieved from http://www.ysu.am/faculties/en/.../section/structure

Moore, J. L., Dickson-Deane, C., & Galyen, K. (2010). E-learning, online learning, and distance education: Are they the same?: e-Learning, online learning, and distance learning environments: Are they the same? *The Internet and Higher Education, 14*, 129–135. doi:10.1016/j.iheduc.2010.10.001

Moore, M. G., & Kearsley, G. (2012). *Distance education: A systems view of online learning*. Belmont, CA: Wadsworth.

National Center for Supercomputing Applications. (2000). E-learning—A review of literature. Retrieved from http://learning.ncsa.uiuc.edu/papers/elearnlit.pdf

National Tempus Offices. (2014). National Tempus Offices in our partner countries: Armenia. (2007–2013). European Commission. Education. Audiovisual and Culture Executive Agency. Retrieved from http://eacea.ec.europa.eu/tempus/participating_countries/armenia_en.php

Orellana, A., Hudgins, T. L., & Simonson, M. (Eds.). (2009). *The perfect online course. Best practices for designing and teaching*. Charlotte, NC: Information Age.

Russian-Armenian (Slavonic) University. (2016). About Russian- Armenian (Slavonic) University. Retrieved from http://www.rau.am/eng/271/2462

Saba, F. (2011). Distance education in the United States: Past, present, future. *Educational Technology, 6*(11), 11–18.

Simonson, M., Smaldino, S., Albright, M., & Zvacek, S. (2012). *Teaching and learning at a distance: Foundations of distance education* (5th ed.). New York, NY: Pearson.

Sorensen, C., & Baylen, D. (2009). Learning online: Adapting the seven principles of good practice to a web-based instructional environment. In A. Orellana, T. L. Hudgins, & M. Simonson, (Eds.), *The perfect online course. Best practices for designing and teaching* (pp. 69–86). Charlotte, NC: Information Age.

Tacis Project in Armenia. (2000). Retrieved from http://www.iatc.am/projects/distance.htm

Yerevan State University. (2007). Information Technologies Educational and Research Centre. Science Infrastructures. Retrieved from http://www.ysu.am/science/en/1350282102

Zawacki-Richter, O., & Kourotchkina, A. (2012). The development of distance education in the Russian Federation and the former Soviet Union. *The International Review of Research in Open and Distance Learning, 13*(3), 165–184. (EJ1001018)

Volume 17, Number 1, 2016

Quarterly Review of Distance Education

RESEARCH THAT GUIDES PRACTICE

Editors:
Michael Simonson
Charles Schlosser

IAP
INFORMATION AGE
PUBLISHING

An Official Journal of the
Association for Educational Communications and Technology

QUARTERLY REVIEW OF DISTANCE EDUCATION,
SUBSCRIBE TODAY!
WWW.INFOAGEPUB.COM

Mental Health in the Online College Classroom

Are Distance Learners Getting the Support They Need for the Challenges They Face?

Marianne Raley

The existing literature about distance learners points to significant struggles with anxiety, isolation, risk of attrition, and other stressors present on the degree path for this vulnerable group, but does not substantially address the possible attendant mental health risks or how to build in mental health support for this unique community of learners. Due to the demographics of adult students who are more likely to attend online college courses, the unique challenges of coping with an online classroom, and the consistent strain of juggling multiple roles inside and outside of the classroom, learners may experience an increase in mental health challenges that can prohibit long-term success and college degree completion (Barr, 2014; Brock, 2014; Hetzel, 2012).

In the fall of 2012, more than 5 million students in the United States were enrolled in online college courses (U.S. Department of Education, 2014). With increasing enrollments and greater university investments in distance learning, more students all over the world will pursue their college degrees exclusively or in part from their phones, tablets, and laptops (Afsari-Mamagani, 2014). While the reach of distance education is growing, so are the kinds of students who take online courses (Kaifi, Mujtaba, & Williams, 2009). Many students who choose online coursework are first generation college students, working or stay at home parents, active military, veterans, older workers who have been out of school for decades, as well as the traditional aged students who may or may not have taken gap year(s) before pursuing or returning to a college degree path (Marcia, 2004). This diverse group of students face

Marianne Raley,
University of Phoenix, 1625 W. Fountainhead Pkwy. CF-S807 Tempe, AZ 85282.
Telephone: (602) 713-7994.
E-mail: marianne.raley@phoenix.edu

many obstacles to completing their degrees and have very high attrition rates, so they require tailored instruction and comprehensive support to keep them engaged with a successful degree path (Kaifi et al., 2009).

Online college modalities may have a wide appeal, but they require a specific skill set for success. Many students who embark on online college course work are underprepared for the demands of the classes and, often, do not have an adequate support system among family and friends who are not in college (Shea & Bidjerano, 2014). The necessary strategies for online college course success include autonomously managing time and assignments without the face-to-face reminder of a brick-and-mortar classroom or physical presence of an instructor; the ability to juggle student life and expectations with professional and personal demands; and the ever-present challenge of navigating the technology—both hardware and software—issues that inevitably arise (Rath, Rock, & Laferriere, 2013). These stressors can create feelings of isolation, disengagement from social communities, and general anxiety, which are widely associated with negative health impacts such as depression (Cornwell & Waite, 2009). The stress, disconnection, and technical difficulties associated with the online classroom require unique accommodation and understanding from instructors, technical staff, and the college at large in which they are enrolled (Rothweiler, 2012). Yet, without a face-to-face presence, it can be extremely difficult to identify and accommodate students who may be struggling with the successful acclimation to the online classroom (Barr, 2014).

Students who access online course work are more likely to be members of minority groups and/or have low incomes, which can increase the likelihood of experiencing mental illness (Bar, 2014). "Robust, entirely online degree programs and services act as an entry point to higher education for typically at-risk students" (Brock, 2014, p. 3). These at-risk learners disproportionately include first generation students who are the first in their family to attend college (Priebe, Ross, & Low, 2008). They often have stubbornly low college completion rates (Pontes & Pontes, 2012). Learners who are "first-generation, low-income college students experience both isolation and marginalization, especially during their first year of college, which impacts their long-term persistence in higher education" (Jehangir, 2009, p. 33). The experience of being the first one in a family to attend college can potentially heighten the incidence of anxiety about academic performance and the pressure to succeed. "Unless people have been through higher education, they do not understand the nuances for getting accepted and graduating from college" (Graham, 2011, p. 3). This can impact the understanding of time management, course navigation, and even how and when to ask questions (Mann, 2005).

Many students who return to or begin college and choose a distance learning degree path may be older workers or those with limited access and facility with the technology required to successfully complete assignments (Sivakumaran & Lux, 2011). They may feel uncertain about using the technology successfully (Rothweiler, 2012). Some research shows that while taking some or all of coursework online can be an aid to degree completion, the adaptation to an online learning environment is challenging for many learners (Griffin & Minter, 2013; Shea & Bidjerano, 2014). An involved teacher who understands the needs and communicates readily with anxious learners can help to promote confidence and reduce feelings of insecurity (Rothweiler, 2012).

Students may experience additional difficulties due to a lack of access to regular Internet connectivity and the necessary hardware to complete assignments (Turpin, 2007). If students have used computers and technology only for work, they may struggle with the basic navigation of any online learning platform or assignment (Turpin, 2007). The "students in lower socioeconomic communities tend to have more limited access on older equipment in their schools and libraries, and the only home access, if at all, is via cell phone" (Griffin & Minter, 2013, p. 146). While many universities are broadening access to online course work through apps that can be used on phones or tablets, these technologies are still evolving (Vázquez-Cano, 2014). Students may have access to smart phones, but at this time, using these devices may not be equivalent to the ease with which a more affluent student may complete work using a current computer with up-to-date software. Though some students readily adapt to the technology requirements, those who do not may feel stress and discomfort when interacting with the online learning platforms. "For students who feel intimidated by technology, learning both course contents and the technology in unison can be a daunting task" (Sivakumaran & Lux, 2011, p. 156). When they experience high levels of confusion by encountering seemingly incomprehensible directions for completing assignments and discussion requirements, they may be more likely to disengage from the classroom and experience stress and anxiety (Sivakumaran & Lux, 2011). Facilitators can help to ease student anxiety by clearly defining expectations and maintaining class routines (Macheski, Lowney, Burhmann, & Bush, 2008). "If older students are guided in the right direction and encouraged to recognize the value behind learning how to use a computer, then they will be more inclined to learn" (Sivakumaran & Lux, 2011, p. 159).

General isolation and disengagement from the classroom and the college add to the challenges that online learners experience. "Students in distance education may experience limited contact with academic staff at the university and department which can contribute to a feeling of disconnectedness" (Bolliger & Inan, 2012, p. 43). They may feel unsupported when they run into the inevitable technical glitch or curriculum issue and they may experience a lack of community when interacting with classmates (Jacqueline & Haycock, 2014). While major life transitions are often accompanied by stress and anxiety, students who experience the greatest stress transitioning to college have the highest needs for quality social interaction. Beneficial social support that aid students during this time are specifically "high quality, high contact relationships that consist of participation in complex social groups" (Galatzer-Levy, Burton, & Bonanno, 2012, p. 562). This disengagement and disconnection from any sense of community can lead to absences, late work, and confusion that can prohibit student success and retention (Golden, 2011).

Complex social groups may be difficult to feel a part of if a student experiences isolation and anxiety in the learning environment and the college overall. As online instruction evolves, there are more opportunities to collaborate in an online classroom, and many courses integrate team projects and collaborative learning tools to help students become more engaged with the learning community. The successful implementation of these new technologies and learning strategies necessitates that the online learner receives targeted support from a well-trained staff in order to "not merely mirror face-to-face practices but leverage the affordances of emerging technologies" (Griffin & Minter, 2013, p. 157). While the new technologies and approaches can make learning more collaborative, students who already have a baseline anxiety with the online classroom or digital resources may not be able to overcome these challenges without significant support from the instructor and college support staff (Rothweiler, 2012).

Students entering college who already have mental health concerns such as social anxiety may experience even more challenges than the average learner. They may be unable to cope with the demands of college. "Social anxiety also negatively affects other aspects of college life, such as academic performance and persistence" (Nordstrom, Goguen, & Hiester, 2014, p. 49). The incidence of anxiety can prevent them from doing their best work or staying with a class to completion (Clair, 2015). Students with a previous diagnosis of anxiety may choose the online learning format as a seemingly safe choice, but are ultimately "at significant risk for social and emotional problems during their first semester and for institutional dropout by their 2nd year" (Nordstrom, Goguen, & Hiester, 2014). Similarly, at-risk populations such as those struggling with posttraumatic stress disorder (PTSD) or traumatic brain injury, as may be found with military or veteran student populations, may experience additional risk for difficulties in the classroom, and ultimately, attrition (Smith-Osborne, 2012). Military members who served in the Iraq/Afghanistan conflicts experienced higher levels of blast-related injuries and therefore are more at risk for symptoms of traumatic brain injury and posttraumatic stress disorder that can inhibit their ability to adjust to the requirements of the classroom (Smee, Buenrostro, Garrick, Sreenivasan, & Weinberger, 2013). Posttraumatic stress disorder and traumatic brain injury symptoms can include "headache, balance problems, nausea, fatigue, sensitivity to noise, irritability, sadness, nervousness, visual problems, and difficulty concentrating and remembering," which can be particularly challenging when navigating environments such as a classroom where concentration and memory are necessary for success (Yeh et al., 2014, p. 2655).

Whether it is anxiety about returning to school after years in the workplace; juggling multiple roles as spouse, employee, parent, and student; working through previously existing mental health conditions; or just managing confusion about software, hardware, or technological requirements of assignment directions, attending college as an adult learner can be a significant challenge. These difficulties are increased when the modality of learning is online and a student must surmount obstacles without the in-person guidance and cues from other classmates or an instructor. First generation college students, minority students, and students with low income face additional stress and challenges accessing the classroom and maintaining confidence about their academic progress. Adult learners may experience greater levels of mental health concerns such as anxiety when attempting to complete a degree in the online classroom (Sivakumaran & Lux, 2011). They may require a specialized effort from faculty and staff to identify problems and help them overcome issues and prevent disengagement (Macheski et al., 2008). These additional layers of challenge and isolation can inhibit success and prevent successful adjustment to the college that they attend. Feelings of isolation, lack of community, technological struggles, and absence of face-to-face assistance can exacerbate doubts and anxiety about the ability to complete college level course work. These pressures can lead to depression, lack of confidence, and ultimately, attrition. Faculty and staff at schools with online courses should be aware of the unique hurdles that distance learners face and be prepared to offer tailored assistance that can help the student through the obstacles so that they can complete their degree program (Barr, 2014).

REFERENCES

Afsari-Mamagani, G. (2014). Hybrid identities & MOOCS: The implications of massive open online courses for multicultural civic education. *Multicultural Education, 21*(2), 2–8.

Barr, B. B. (2014). Identifying and addressing the mental health needs of online students in higher education. *Online Journal of Distance Learning Administration, 17*(2), 35–40.

Bolliger, D. U., & Inan, F. A. (2012). Development and validation of the online student connectedness survey (OSCS). *International Review of Research in Open and Distance Learning, 13*(3), 41–65.

Brock, K. R. (2014). *Identifying the factors that predict degree completion for entirely online community college students* (Order No. 3613846). Available from ProQuest Dissertations & Theses Full Text. (1513243695)

Clair, D. S. (2015). A simple suggestion for reducing first-time online student anxiety. *Journal of Online Learning and Teaching, 11*(1), 129.

Cornwell, E. Y., & Waite, L. J. (2009). Social disconnectedness, perceived isolation, and health among older adults. *Journal of Health and Social Behavior, 50*(1), 31–48.

Galatzer-Levy, I., Burton, C. L., & Bonanno, G. A. (2012). Coping flexibility, potentially traumatic life events, and resilience: A prospective study of college student adjustment. *Journal of Social and Clinical Psychology, 31*(6), 542–567. doi:http://dx.doi.org/101521jscp2012316542

Graham, L. (2011). Learning a new world: Reflections on being a first-generation college student and the influence of TRIO programs. *New Directions for Teaching & Learning, 2011*(127), 33–38. doi:10.1002/tl.455

Griffin, J., & Minter, D. (2013). The rise of the online writing classroom: Reflecting on the material conditions of college composition teaching. *College Composition and Communication, 65*(1), 140–161.

Golden, D. R. (2011). *Students and teachers; perceptions of "community" in online college composition* (Order No. 3460536). Available from ProQuest Central; ProQuest Dissertations & Theses Full Text. (877974441)

Hetzel, L. C. (2012). *How multiple roles influence adult college women's online student experiences in a rural community college context* (Order No. 3548396). Available from ProQuest Dissertations & Theses Full Text. (1270798038)

Jacqueline, A. B., & Haycock, J. (2014). Roles and student identities in online large course forums: Implications for practice. *International Review of Research in Open and Distance Learning, 15*(1), 20–40.

Jehangir, R. R. (2009). Cultivating voice: First-generation students seek full academic citizenship in multicultural learning communities. *Innovative Higher Education, 34*(1), 33–49

Kaifi, B. A., Mujtaba, B. G., & Williams, A. A. (2009). Online college education for computer-savvy students: A study of perceptions and needs. *Journal of College Teaching and Learning, 6*(6), 1–15.

Macheski, G. E., Lowney, K. S., Buhrmann, J., & Bush, M. E. (2008). Overcoming student disengagement and anxiety in theory, methods, and statistics courses by building a community of learners. *Teaching Sociology, 36*(1), 42–48.

Mann, S. J. (2005). Alienation in the learning environment: A failure of community? *Studies in Higher Education, 30*(1), 43–55.

Marcia, P. H. (2004). Teaching in our pajamas: Negotiating with adult learners in online distance writing courses. *College Teaching, 52*(2), 58–62.

Nordstrom, A. H., Goguen, L. S., & Hiester, M. (2014). The effect of social anxiety and self-esteem on college adjustment, academics, and retention. *Journal of College Counseling, 17*(1), 48–63.

Pontes, F., & Pontes N., (2012). Distance education enrollment Is associated with greater academic progress among first generation low-income undergraduate students in the US in 2008. *Online Journal of Distance Learning Administration, 15*(1).

Priebe, L. C., Ross, T. L., & Low, K. W. (2008). Exploring the role of distance education in fostering equitable university access for first generation students: A phenomenological survey. *International Review of Research in Open and Distance Learning, 9*(1), 1–12.

Rath, B., Rock, K., & Laferriere, A. (2013). *Pathways through college: Strategies for improving community college student success.* Hartford, CT: Our Piece of the Pie.

Rothweiler, B. M. (2012). *Factors related to successful course completion in an online program for returning high school dropouts* (Order No. 3527249). Available from ProQuest Dissertations & Theses Full Text. (1082007589)

Shea, P., & Bidjerano, T. (2014). Does online learning impede degree completion? A national study of community college students. *Computers & Education, 75*, 103–111.

Sivakumaran, T., & Lux, A. C. (2011, September). Overcoming computer anxiety: A three-step process for adult learners. *US-China Education Review, B, 1,* 155–161.

Smee, D., Buenrostro, S., Garrick, T., Sreenivasan, S., & Weinberger, L. E. (2013). Combat to college: Cognitive fatigue as a challenge in Iraq and Afghanistan war veterans with traumatic brain injury: Pilot study survey results. *Journal of Applied Rehabilitation Counseling, 44*(4), 25–33.

Smith-Osborne, A. (2012). Supported education for returning veterans with PTSD and other mental disorders. *Journal of Rehabilitation, 78*(2), 4–12.

Turpin, C. A. (2007). Feminist praxis, online teaching, and the urban campus. *Feminist Teacher, 18*(1), 9–27. doi:10.1353/ftr.2008.0017

U.S. Department of Education, National Center for Education Statistics. (2014). *Enrollment in distance education courses, by state: Fall 2012* (NCES 2014-023). Retrieved from https://nces.ed.gov/fastfacts/display.asp?id=80

Vázquez-Cano, E. (2014). Mobile distance learning with smartphones and apps in higher education. *Kuram Ve Uygulamada Egitim Bilimleri, 14*(4), 1505–1520.

Yeh, P., Wang, B., Oakes, T. R., French, L. M., Pan, H., Graner, J., & ... Riedy, G. (2014). Postconcussional disorder and PTSD symptoms of military-related traumatic brain injury associated with compromised neurocircuitry. *Human Brain Mapping, 35*(6), 2652–2673. doi:10.1002/hbm.22358

Orientation Programs to Increase Retention in Online Community College Courses

Wendy Robichaud

INTRODUCTION

Learning is part of human nature, but formal learning is not always intuitive and needs guidance. This is especially true for learning at a distance. As the need for education increases, distance education is becoming a way to meet the growing demand (Hachey, Conway, & Wladis, 2013). Currently, 83.6% of colleges with 1,000–4,999 students offer distance/online courses (Allen & Seaman, 2015). One definition of distance education is "institution-based, formal education where the learning group is separated, and where interactive telecommunications systems are used to connect learners, resources, and instructors" (Simonson, Smaldino, Albright, & Zvacek, 2012, p. 32). Teaching online is not as simple as posting a syllabus and videotaped lectures on a website; there should be intentional instructional design to transition a course from face to face to distance (Ko & Rossen, 2010). The basic day-to-day activities such as interactions between instructors and students or students and students; course handouts and syllabi; assignment submissions and assessments; and how to ask questions are different than in the traditional face-to-face classroom. For these reasons, instructors are expected to have pedagogical training as well as technical training to teach online courses at a distance (Ekstrand, 2012). Students must be shown how to navigate this kind of classroom too. Students need to be guided in order to know what is expected and those expectations need to be clearly articulated in more than one location (Simonson et al., 2012). Student support services and administrators must address the distance student's specific needs by orienting students to this different type of classroom and format of

Wendy Robichaud,
Teacher, Oxford Hills Technical School,
256 Main Street, South Paris, ME 04281.
Telephone: (207) 743-7756 x5100.
E-mail: w.robichaud@msad17.org

learning. This should address everything from technical issues and the technical requirements of online learning, to course expectations, etiquette, and course procedures (Ko & Rossen, 2010).

ONLINE EDUCATION

Reports from higher education institutions claim there is an increased demand for online courses over face-to-face courses (Allen & Seaman, 2010). Even though there is still resistance from faculty (who question the validity of online learning), more than 70.8% of chief academic leaders say that online learning must be part of their strategic planning (Allen & Seaman, 2015). Although distance education and online courses can be seen as a delivery method offering greater availability of education, there is a price associated with this increased access. Distance education is speculated to have lower completion rates and higher attrition rates than face-to-face courses. Retention is a concern because student failure can lead to less chance of enrolling in future courses, whereas student success increases these chances (Simonson et al., 2012). Currently, 7.1 million students are enrolling in online courses and 35.5% of all students have taken at least one online course in their career (Allen & Seaman, 2014). Considering these figures, retention for online courses needs to be a focus for administrators and student support services. Retention rates for distance education are cited as being much lower than their face-to-face counterparts (Gascoigne & Parnell, 2014; Taylor, Dunn, & Winn, 2015). There are many factors listed for these attrition rates, ranging from underestimating the time commitment involved in online learning to the difficulty of the courses (technical and subject matter). If the increase in enrollment of distance courses continues, then retention of students in these programs must be a priority.

COMMUNITY COLLEGE

Enrollment at community colleges continues to grow. President Obama's proposed initiative to expand community college graduation rates to 5 million by 2020 means this increase will continue (Obama, 2010). The greater demand on community colleges is being met by offering online courses. In fact, approximately 61% of all community college students have taken an online course (Pearson Foundation, 2011). The increase in students taking online courses, combined with the research indicating that attrition rates are higher for online courses, is a cause for concern (Hachey et al., 2013). Community college students are already at greater risk of attrition in on-campus, face-to-face courses. Community college students are often considered nontraditional students with fulltime jobs, children, and commitments (Hachey et al., 2013). According to the research, nontraditional students are at greater risk of noncompletion (Rovai & Downey, 2010). Nontraditional students tend to be older, may be first-generation college students, attend college part time, work, or be from minority populations. These nontraditional students often take advantage of online courses because they require less time commuting or actually sitting in class. Their reasons for attrition range from work and family commitments to being unprepared for college in general (Hachey et al., 2013). These are the students most at risk of dropping out (Pearson Foundation, 2011). This means community college students taking online courses should be a focus for retention interventions and suggestions.

RETENTION SUGGESTIONS

There are a host of studies surrounding retention dating back to as early as the 1800s (Hachey et al., 2013). These studies suggest that there are many factors affecting attrition and retention. Some of these reasons may be out of anyone's control;

however, a few of them may be within the control of college administrators. Misunderstandings of the time and effort involved to complete an online course; having the skills for dealing with the technical aspects of online learning; the quality of interactions and relationships with faculty and peers; and the areas of grading, feedback, and communication are all aspects where administrators can work to improve student success (Cho, 2012; Karp & Bork, 2012). Administrators can provide guidance for both students and faculty to improve the learning experience. Also in these studies, suggestions for overcoming attrition and increasing retention included expanding the types of support systems offered to students, such as intervention and advising, and communicating high expectations (Hart, 2012). Likewise, giving students a way to acclimate to school and providing a sense of community were suggestions to encourage success (Cole, Shelley, & Swartz, 2014). These suggestions are especially true for online students, where there is a greater feeling of detachment. (Ekstrand, 2012; Rovai & Downey, 2010) Lastly, bolstering the quality of interactions between faculty and students, gaining faculty acceptance of online learning, and testing student's autonomy are also ways to raise retention rates (Ekstrand, 2012). Many of these suggestions can be part of an orientation that administrators use to help guide students as they begin taking courses. Adequately preparing students for online learning should be the first step to ensuring their success.

The special population of community college students requires attention too. The Pearson Foundation (2011) suggested community college students do not feel their high school experiences adequately prepare them for college courses. Research shows that this preparation is not simply academic related, but also the behaviors of the students such as skills, attitudes, and habits. These behaviors can be guided by setting students' expectations before they begin school (Karp & Bork, 2012). This guidance is necessary for many students and can be provided by the college to help them understand how to be a college student. Students need to know how to be organized, how to study, and how to be proactive in advocating for themselves. Communication can be a barrier, but it can be overcome by clearly setting expectations and explaining unspoken rules and roles to students. The expectations, as well as the role the student plays in the learning process, can be unknown to students and often misunderstood. An orientation is one way to set clear expectations and help students understand their role as a student (Karp & Bork, 2102). The orientation should address the issues of study habits, communication, and time management, as well as the basics of online learning, navigating the specific course management systems, and assessing overall readiness for learning online (Cho, 2012).

THEORETICAL PERSPECTIVE

Theories surrounding attrition and retention span decades and help administrators understand some of the reasons why students do not succeed, as well as provide guidance when looking for ways to help. Tinto (1975) and Bean and Metzner (1985) created models that attempted to explain why some students were successful. Tinto focused on two factors: social and academic integration. He theorized that successful persistence involved individual characteristics and experiences prior to college along with experiences after admission. Tinto called these experiences after admission *integration variables* and broke the variables into two parts: academic experiences and social experiences. He theorized that a student is more likely to persist when he or she is more integrated. He calculated integration by grade point average and the frequency of positive interactions with peers and faculty. Rovai (2003) wrote that Tinto's theory was somewhat limited for explaining the persistence of nontraditional students because they often do not have the same integration. Bean and Metzner's model added features that describe the persistence of nontraditional students. The model helps explain the characteristics of students older than 24, who do not live on campus, attend part time, and gain support mostly outside the institution. Rovai (2003) said Bean and Metzner's model was more appropriate for explaining the persistence of students learning at a distance. Their theory incorporated more of the environmental influences effecting nontraditional distance students such as employment and family responsibilities. The Bean and Metzner model was divided into variables called academic outcomes and psychological outcomes. Several models use a combination of these two theories to create more holistic approaches. Rovai (2003) merged the two theories for his model of student persistence. Rovai (2003) created a new model to explain student persistence in online distance education programs, which combined student characteristics and skills prior to admissions with external and internal factors affecting students after admission. Rovai (2003) recognized that there is no simple formula for success and that many factors are involved in a student's desire to persist.

Rovai (2003) created a category called factors prior to admissions which combined student characteristics, both demographics and academic performance, with student skills. He merged external and internal factors mentioned by Tinto (1975) and Bean and Metzner (1985) with students' needs and pedagogy to create a classification called factors after admission. These factors all affect a student's decision to persist in a course. Using Rovai's theory, the idea of using an orientation as a means of encouraging success for online community college students makes sense. A comprehensive orientation is the beginning of integration (social and academic), establishes the skills necessary for success, and promotes self-efficacy/autonomy. Figure 1 details the information in Rovai's model of his theory.

ORIENTATION PROGRAMS

Studies have shown that students drop out for reasons that may be divided into three categories: factors related to students, factors related to courses or programs, and environmental factors (Lee & Choi, 2011). Factors related to students included academic background and grade point average, relevant academic experiences, skills, and study habits. Factors related to courses or programs included the design of the course, institutional supports, and interactions in the course with faculty and peers. Environmental factors included family commitments, work commitments, and the presence of external support. In fact, 75% of the reasons why students drop out can be resolved by having a greater understanding of students' challenges and by providing well-structured supports. Many of the specific factors listed earlier can be addressed by the school, at least partially, thus helping to reduce attrition rates. Some examples of strategies to promote retention include offering an orientation, providing academic advising throughout the semester, offering computer training, assessing student readiness before they begin courses, offering a cohort, and utilizing tutors (Hart, 2012; Lee & Choi, 2011). The orientation itself can even include several of these suggestions. Clearly, the best way to increase retention is to add several of these strategies. However, the orientation can be a first step that combines factors like assessing readiness with training and advising.

Several factors are important for a quality orientation program. The orientation must be easy to use, must be offered at the right time, and must be specific to the learning management system (LMS) being used. Basic information such as an intro-

Prior to Admission

Student Characteristics
(Tinto and Bean & Metzner)
Age, Ethnicity & Gender
Intellectual Development
Academic Performance
Academic Preparation

Student Skills
Computer Literacy
Information Literacy
Time Management
Reading & Writing
Computer-based Interaction

After Admission

External Factors
(Bean & Metzner)
Finances
Hours of Employment
Family Responsibilities
Outside Encouragement
Opportunity to Transfer
Life Crises

Internal Factors

(Tinto)
Academic Integration
Social Integration
Goal Commitment
Institutional Commitment
Learning Community

(Bean & Metzner)
Study Habits
Advising
Absenteeism
Course Availability
Program Fit
Current GPA
Utility
Stress
Satisfaction
Commitment

Student Needs
Clarity of Programs
Self-Esteem
Identification with School
Interpersonal Relationships
Accessibility to Services

Pedagogy
Learning Styles
Teaching Styles

Persistence Decision

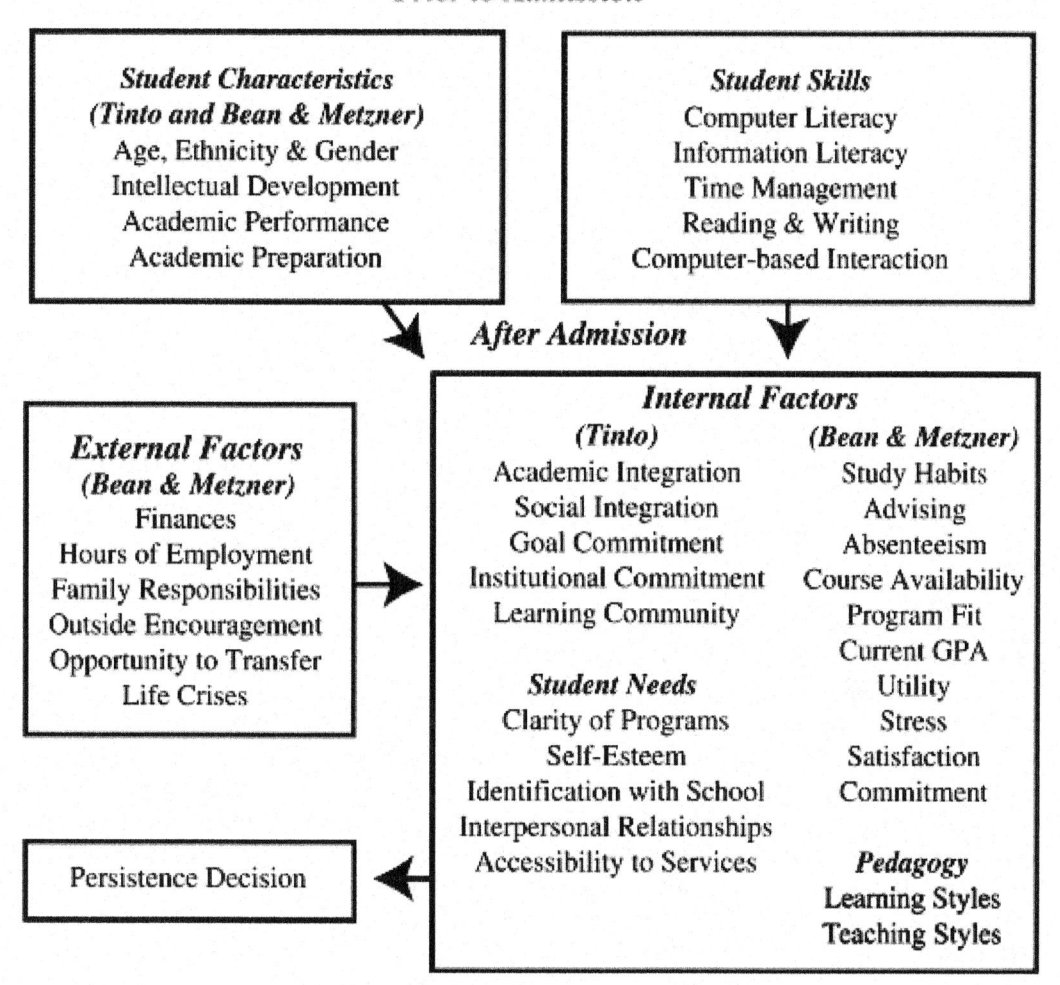

Figure 1. A conceptualization of Rovai's (2003) composite persistence model (p. 9).

duction to the campus, registrar, financial aid, the library, and key personnel are great, but not enough. Some important factors to include are: a clear communication of the expectations of the student (everything from assignment due dates to how many words should be in a discussion post), clear instructions on using the LMS (where to turn in assignments, where to find information, etc.), a chance to work out technology barriers (interacting with the LMS before class starts), and how the course and its materials are organized (Harris, Larrier, & Castano-Bishop, 2011;

Karp & Bork, 2012). By discussing two models, a much clearer idea of how to implement a comprehensive orientation, using Rovai's (2003) persistence model, can be understood. Neither model was designed specifically for community college students, but both have qualities that would be useful to that particular demographic.

ORIENTATION EXAMPLES

Taylor et al. (2015) implemented an orientation for online courses that helped raise the success rate of several courses. The orientation was made available to a few courses that either had a high dropout rate, were often the first online course students enrolled in, or were seen as having high enrollment. The orientation consisted of videos embedded into the courses on the LMS and covered: how to get started, basic navigation, how to post in discussion threads, how to submit assignments, and how to check grades and instructor feedback. Two pieces of this orientation stood out. First, the videos were interactive and allowed for students to check their learning. Second, the videos were left in the LMS for the duration of the course. This left the video as a "just-in-time" asset for students that needed to review the video at any time during the course (Taylor et al., 2015). This feature helped students have information on demand in multiple locations, as advised by Simonson et al. (2012).

Cho (2012) designed a four-part orientation that included: the nature of online learning, how to use the course management system, the technical requirements of an online course, and the learning skills and motivation required for online learning. The four parts were set up into modules, each allowing users to navigate through the course management system. Short videos and tutorials were followed by short quizzes to ensure students understood the material. The first module discussed the expectations of the students, how to communicate to faculty and other students, time management, and how to seek help and resources. The second module discussed the specifics of the LMS, how to navigate it, and how to turn in assignments and add discussion posts. The third module went over various technical requirements, but kept the information basic. The last module of the orientation consisted of a short self-assessment test for students to take stock of their understanding of the learning skills and motivation necessary to complete an online course. The key features of this orientation (besides the tutorials on how to use the particular LMS) were the background knowledge it gave students and the self-assessments students took to understand what traits they needed to succeed. The background helped set student expectations and the self-assessment makes students reflect before committing to online learning.

Both orientations use elements of Rovai's (2003) persistence model. Taylor et al. (2015) focused on student skills such as computer literacy and information literacy. They also tried to relieve some stress by making the videos accessible throughout the course, which also counts toward a type of advising and accessibility to services. Both orientations help students feel welcome and help with academic integration. Cho (2012) focused on making students aware of the commitment online learning requires, as well as time management and study habits. His orientation even mentions the distractions that external factors can pose on learning and some tips to avoid those pitfalls. Both orientations are useful examples of how students can be guided as they begin their online journey. However, these are just two examples. Many more exist and are worthy of exploring. There is no "correct" way to organize the orientation. It should be a comprehensive combination of materials that will guide students and increase success (Cho, 2012; Taylor et al., 2015)

CONCERNS

Orientations are one way to give distance students an introduction to what online learning is and some skills necessary to succeed. However, orientations are not mandatory everywhere, for every student. Some programs or colleges only offer voluntary orientations for online students enrolled in fully online programs. What happens to students not fully enrolled in an online program? Students who take one online course during their degree or students who are not matriculated and take just one online course may not have access to an orientation. These students may fall through the proverbial crack. If studies show that orientations increase retention, should they be mandatory for every student before enrolling in an online course of any kind? These questions can only be answered through further research on both student retention in general and orientations themselves.

Orientations are not the only answer. As previously mentioned, other strategies include high quality academic advising, computer training, assessing student readiness, offering a cohort, and utilizing tutors (Hart, 2012; Lee & Choi, 2011). More research needs to be conducted on the value of orientations, along with these other strategies to determine what elements offer the most promising results for increasing retention. Additionally, more studies need to focus on the special characteristics of community college students taking online courses and how those characteristics influence retention and attrition.

CONCLUSION

The problem of retention in online courses, specifically community college online courses, needs to be given attention. As colleges offer more online courses and enrollment increases, strategies must be implemented to encourage the successful completion of these courses. Online orientations are one way to promote success. Actively trying to prepare students for the unique nature of online learning, orienting students to the LMS, and giving students an adequate idea of the expectations in an online course are just some of the benefits an orientation can provide. Orientations should be constructed using theoretical perspectives such as the Rovai (2003) model of persistence theory and it may be necessary to make them mandatory. An orientation is not the only answer to retention issues, but it is one piece of the puzzle that can increase success. A mandatory orientation before enrolling in an online course is a concrete step administrators can take toward improving retention rates. There is no correct way to organize an orientation, but a comprehensive, mandatory guide tailored to the individual college, which is accessed by all students before beginning their first online course is an asset and a viable way to increase retention and success.

REFERENCES

Allen, I. E., & Seaman, J. (2010). Class differences: Online education in the United States. Retrieved from http://www.onlinelearningsurvey.com/highered.html

Allen, I. E., & Seaman, J. (2014). Grade change: Tracking online education in the United States. Retrieved from http://www.onlinelearningsurvey.com/reports/gradechange.pdf

Allen, I. E., & Seaman, J. (2015). Grade change: Tracking online education in the United States. Retrieved from http://www.onlinelearningsurvey.com/reports/gradelevel.pdf

Bean, J. P., & Metzner, B. S. (1985). A conceptual model of nontraditional undergraduate student attrition. *Review of Educational Research, 55*, 485–540. doi:10.2307/1170245

Cho, M-H. (2012). Online student orientation in higher education: A developmental study. *Educational Technology Research & Development, 60*(6), 1051–1069. doi:10.1007/s11423-012-9271-4

Cole, M. T., Shelley, D. J., & Swartz, L. B. (2014). Online instruction, e-learning, and student satisfaction: A three year study. *International Review of Research in Open & Distance Learning, 15*(6), 111–131.

Ekstrand, B. (2013). Prerequisites for persistence in distance education. *Online Journal of Distance Learning Administration, 16*(2). Retrieved from http://www.westga.edu/~distance/ojdla/fall163/ekstrand164.html

Gascoigine, C., & Parnell, J. (2014). Distance education readiness assessments: An overview and application *Online Journal of Distance Learning Administration, 17*(4).

Retrieved from http://www.westga.edu/~distance/ojdla/winter174/gascoigne_parnell174.html

Hachey, A. C., Conway, K. M., & Wladis, C. W. (2013). Community colleges and underappreciated assets: Using institutional data to promote success in online learning. *Online Journal of Distance Learning Administration, 16*(1), 1–18.

Harris, S. M., Larrier, Y. I., & Castano-Bishop, M. (2011). Development of the student expectations of online learning survey (SEOLS): A pilot study. *Online Journal of Distance Learning Administration, 14*(4), 6–6.

Hart, C. (2012). Factors associated with student persistence in an online program of study: A review of the literature. *Journal of Interactive Online Learning, 11*(1), 19–42.

Karp, M. M., & Bork, R. H. (2012). "They never told me what to expect, so I didn't know what to do": Defining and clarifying the role of a community college student (Vol. CCRC Working Paper No. 47). New York, NY: Columbia University, Teachers College, Community College Research Center.

Ko, S., & Rossen, S. (2010). *Teaching online: A practical guide* (3rd ed.). New York, NY: Routledge.

Lee, Y., & Choi, J. (2011). A review of online course dropout research: Implications for practice and future research. *Educational Technology Research & Development, 59*(5), 593–618. doi:10.1007/s11423-010-9177-y

Obama, B. H. (2010). Remarks at the White House Summit on Community Colleges (pp. 1–5). Washington, DC: Superintendent of Documents.

Pearson Foundation. (2011). *Pearson Foundation community college student survey*. Retrieved from http://www.pearsonfoundation.org/great-learning/partnerships/community-college-survey.html

Rovai, A. P. (2003). In search of higher persistence rates in distance education online programs. *The Internet and Higher Education, 6*(1), 1–16. doi:http://dx.doi.org/10.1016/S1096-7516(02)00158-6

Rovai, A. P., & Downey, J. R. (2010). Why some distance education programs fail while others succeed in a global environment. *The Internet & Higher Education, 13*(3), 141–147. doi:10.1016/j.iheduc.2009.07.001

Simonson, M., Smaldino, S., Albright, M., & Zvacek, S. (2012). *Teaching and learning at a distance: Foundations of distance education* (5th ed.). Boston, MA: Pearson.

Taylor, J. M., Dunn, M., & Winn, S. K. (2015). Innovative orientation leads to improved success in online courses. *Online Learning, 19*(4), 112–120.

Tinto, V. (1975). Dropout from higher education: A theoretical synthesis of recent research. *Review of Educational Research, 45*, 89–125.

USDLA Award Winners 2016

BEST PRACTICES AWARDS FOR DISTANCE LEARNING PROGRAMMING

PLATINUM
LearnBop from Fuel Education
Online Technology ~ K-12 Education

GOLD
t-MBA Digital
(Teenager MBA Academic Program
of Doğa Schools)
Online Technology ~ High School Education

SILVER
Sessions College for Professional Design
Associate of Occupational Studies
in Graphic Design
Online Technology ~ Higher Education

BRONZE
The University of Arkansas System eVersity
Adam Peterson and Crystal Halley, JD
Online Technology ~ Higher Education

BEST PRACTICES AWARDS FOR EXCELLENCE IN DISTANCE LEARNING TEACHING

PLATINUM
Jenna Ellis
Online Technology ~ K-12 Education

GOLD
Greg Zorbas & Rob Sparks
Videoconferencing Technology ~
K–12 Education

SILVER
Dr. James Pappas Oklahoma State University
Online Technology ~ Higher Education

BRONZE
Dr. Julia Carpenter
Online Technology ~ Higher Education

OUTSTANDING LEADERSHIP BY AN INDIVIDUAL IN THE FIELD OF DISTANCE LEARNING

Bharanidharan Rajakumar
CEO, LearnBop
Online Technology ~ K-12 Education

Amanda Ebel
Executive Director,
South Carolina Connections Academy
Online Technology ~ K-12 Education

21ST CENTURY AWARDS FOR BEST PRACTICES IN DISTANCE LEARNING

Stevens Institute of Technology, WebCampus
Online Technology ~ Higher Education

The OWL Team Excelsior College
Online Technology ~ Higher Education

Boston University
Office of Distance Education
Online Technology ~ Higher Education

Master of Industrial Distribution Program
Engineering Technology &
Industrial Distribution
College of Engineering
Texas A&M University
Online Technology–Higher Education

Arizona Telemedicine Program
Online Technology ~
Telemedicine / Higher Education

USDLA 2016 HALL OF FAME
Raymond E. Schroeder,
University of Illinois at Springfield
Hal Plotkin, Creative Commons USA
Michael R. Simonson,
Nova Southeastern University

USDLA 2016 EAGLE AWARD
Commissioner Robert "Bob" Burns
Arizona Corporate Commission

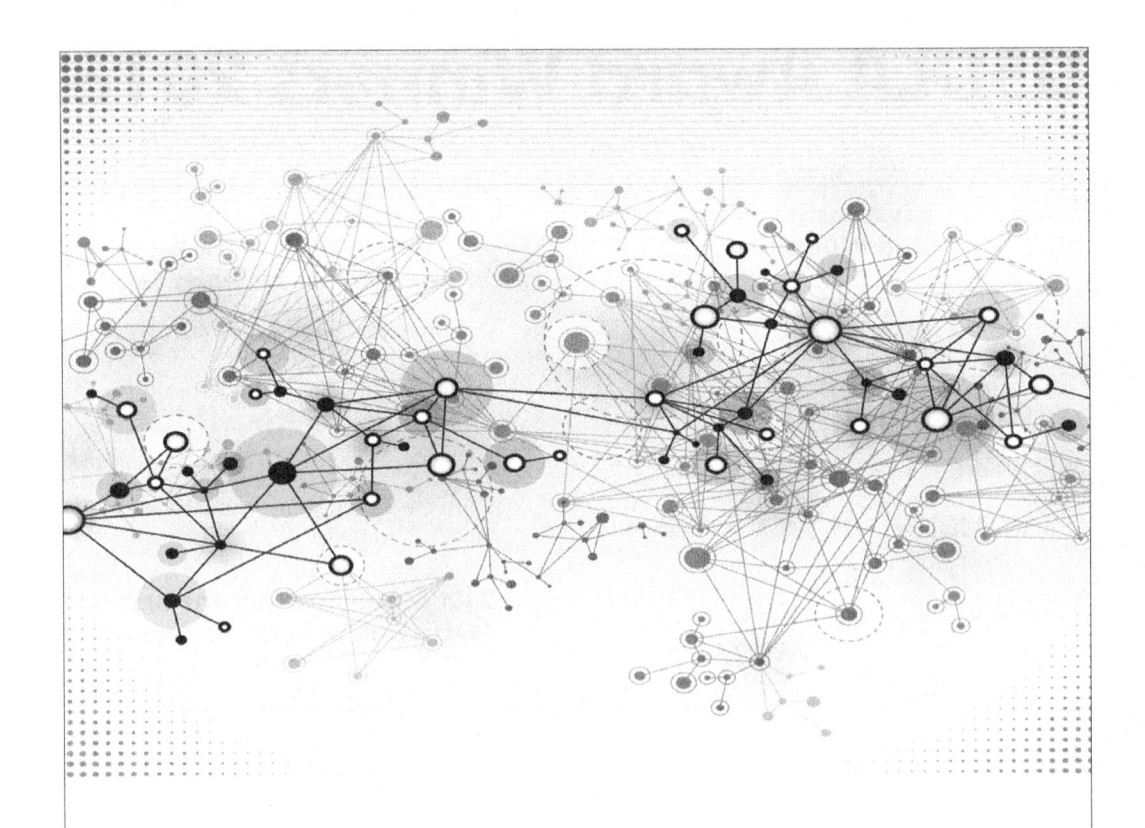

TEACHING AND LEARNING AT A DISTANCE

Foundations of Distance Education

SIXTH EDITION

Michael Simonson

Sharon Smaldino

Susan Zvacek

Get Your Copy Today—Information Age Publishing

Ends and Means

Motivating the Online Learner Using Keller's ARCS Model

Natalie B. Milman and Jeffrey Wessmiller

INTRODUCTION

Several decades ago, Keller developed the Macro model of motivation and performance, the conceptual foundation of the attention, relevance, confidence, satisfaction (ARCS) model of motivation (Keller, 1987, 2010). Some might wonder how a model that dates back to the age of the Apple II computer could remain applicable to today's learners, particularly those who are learning online. The following provides suggestions for ways in which online instructors might incorporate the ARCS model for teaching students in

Natalie B. Milman,
Associate Professor of Educational Technology, The George Washington University, 2134 G ST, NW, Washington, DC 20052.
Telephone: (202) 994-1884.
E-mail: nmilman@gwu.edu

Jeffrey Wessmiller,
Training Specialist,
Telephone: (571) 999-3470.
E-mail: jwessmiller@gmail.com

online environments. Table 1 provides a synopsis of many strategies instructors might wish to employ.

ATTENTION

When someone mentions attention in an instructional design context, it is frequently interpreted as a preliminary step in the learning process limited to the introduction. For example, a student of Gagne (1977) might interpret gaining attention as the first instructional event of nine independent steps in the learning process. Within the ARCS model however, empha-

Table 1. Applying Keller's ARCS Model to Online Learning

ARCS Component	Strategy	Potential Area of Application
Attention	Include activities and assignments that require frequent interaction	Discussion/assignments
	Include visual elements such as videos	Lecture
	Utilize simulations	Assignments
	Vary the style of instruction (font, graphics, etc.)	Lecture
	Encourage debate	Discussion
	Introduce incongruity	Lecture
	Allow students to ask questions of each other	Discussion
	Use questions to peek curiosity	Discussion
	Incorporate humor	Lecture/personal correspondence
Relevance	Base curriculum on real world issues/scenarios	Lecture
	Target content to the learner's needs	Lecture
	Have student's make link between course materials and future goals	Discussion
	Outline objectives	Lecture
	Allow topic choices in activities	Activities
	Implement group work	Activities
	Use student experiences	Discussion
	Use personal pronouns and student names	Personal correspondence
	Provide supplemental information/links	Lecture
	Use guest speaker	Lecture
Confidence	Use a visual appealing professional design to give credibility	Lecture
	Utilize a simple interface	Lecture
	Include practice questions/reviews	Activities
	Provide grading rubrics	Activities
	Establish realistic expectations about requirements for success	Personal correspondence
	Scaffold the course appropriately	Course design
	Identify areas of problematic concern	Personal correspondence
	Allow students to explain their strengths or areas of expertise	Discussion
	Make content challenging but achievable	Course design
	Allow learner to control pace and sequencing	Lecture
Satisfaction	Provide supportive feedback	Personal correspondence
	Reinforce and provide praise	Personal correspondence
	Allow hands-on practice	Activities

Sources: Brennan (2002); Delgran, Vihstadt, and Evans (2015); Huett, Moller, Young, Bray, and Huett (2008); Johnson (2012); Jokelova (2013); Pinchevsky-Font and Dunbar (2015); Schartz, (2014); Taran (2005); Thompson (2016).

sis is placed not only on generating attention, but also sustaining it. Keller (2010) divided attention into three categories: perceptual arousal, inquiry arousal, and variability. The first two are best served to gain attention, while the last is best utilized to maintain it.

Although the first inclination to gain attention might be to use noise or movement, these strategies have limited application in perceptual arousal. Keller (2010) instead suggested involving concreteness and specific people and events to appeal to the learner's emotions. Three potential strategies that are easily applied to online learning include using videos, graphics, and comic strips for gaining attention. An example of the former is the Federal Bureau of Investigation's (2015) *We Regret to Inform You* lesson. The training begins with a video of a mother describing the murder of her young daughter. The powerful testimony evokes empathy and compassion in the learner, which strongly motivates. Alternatively humor might also serve a similar purpose, albeit on the opposite end of the emotional spectrum. For instance, Gorham and Christophel (1990) hypothesized that humor "might be directly related to increased attention, however, it has been difficult to provide consistent empirical evidence that such a direct relationship does exist" (p. 58). When humor is used in perceptual arousal, an elevated understanding of the target audience must exist because it can also be detrimental to the instruction if it distracts too much from the lesson (Wanzer, 2010).

Inquiry arousal can be accomplished by "creating paradoxes, generating inquiries, and nurturing thinking challenges" (Keller, 2010, p. 92). Posing a hypothetical question or scenario are tactics especially applicable to teaching online. Any strategy to encourage curiosity in the learner helps stimulate this type of attention.

Variability can be applied by using different presentation styles and multimedia. Adding a video or activity can accomplish this objective, but Keller (2010) noted that even subtle format changes such as font, spacing, and layout can also help overcome boredom. If the lesson includes narration, consider using different speakers or altering one's speech to emphasize key points, as well as use narration that maintains learners' interest.

RELEVANCE

For adult learners, knowing why they need to learn something before undertaking to learn it is key (Knowles, Holton, & Swanson, 2015). Relevance deals with the perception of whether or not the course/material satisfies personal or career goals of the learners. Keller (2010) advocated relating instructional content to familiar experiences/ideas of the learners. Instructors can incorporate relevance by relating material to current events, which poses an excellent opportunity for an online scavenger hunt activity with this focus (Watkins, 2005). The content being presented might also prove relevant in the pursuit of other learning goals. If the content of one course can be applied to another (i.e., perhaps within a certain program), this can be brought to the learner's attention to increase motivation.

In a study by Frymier and Houser (1998), one of the methods to isolate and test the effects of relevance was to use the second person point of view instead of the third person in certain segments of instruction. By placing the learners in roles as opposed to worked models or examples, students might be more likely to visualize the application of the material, as well as relate to it, and therefore be more motivated to learn it. A mix of hypothetical scenarios and examples might be the best approach to combine the strengths of each.

Another strategy to apply the relevance concept is to share some of the information collected from the needs analysis, if one was conducted. What was the gap that drove instruction? Why was this course developed in the first place? Explaining the goals, objectives, and rationale for learning the content might also help learners comprehend its relevance.

CONFIDENCE

Once you have captured learners' attention and they perceive it is relevant, then the instructor's task is to convince them that they are capable of accomplishing the task at hand. Keller (2010) wrote that "Anxiety and fear are much greater parts of students' lives than teachers realize" (p. 137). This is especially difficult to detect via online learning environments. The objective is to overcome this concern and foster the belief that there is a degree of control and predictability in the learning process.

There are numerous ways in which instructors might build learners' confidence. Instructors can make pep talk videos (what Keller calls "motivational messages") or emphasize textually that students are on the right track and can do it. Instructors can also send targeted e-mail messages to foster building their confidence by emphasizing to students that they are not the first to experience learning this challenging content (i.e., *Others have made it, and so can you!*).

When instructors provide formative feedback, they should emphasize students' strengths, as well as highlight specific ways in which they can grow. Additionally, scaffolding instruction, teaching within their zone of proximal development (Vygotsky, 1978), and checking for understanding are essential for building student confidence.

SATISFACTION

Keller (2010) wrote that intrinsic motivation is one of the most important elements of satisfaction but also the most difficult to influence. Extrinsic motivation, however, is more easily influenced, primarily through the use of feedback. Online learning provides the opportunity for this to be immediate, which is priceless in building confidence. Providing fast recognition of correct answers and good work (even if automated) serves this purpose well. Assessment and grading must be fair and align with stated expectations. Keller (2010) advocated the use of "consistent measurement standards for all learners' tasks and accomplishments" (p. 189). Clear objectives can be supplemented with a rubric to assist in this area.

Newby, Stepich, Lehman, Russell, and Ottenbreit-Leftwich (2012) suggested allowing students to apply what they learn as soon as possible to build motivation through satisfaction. If it is not practical to accomplish this in a performance context, something like allowing learners to showcase their work to other students via a wiki or discussion board is a good substitute.

CONCLUSION

Keller's ARCS Model has many applications in online education. By including the elements of Attention, Relevance, Confidence, and Satisfaction, instructors can increase the motivation of learners even if they are geographically separated and content is taught asynchronously.

REFERENCES

Brennan, W. J. (2002). *Applying Keller's ARCS model of motivation to the design and presentation of web-based courses* (Doctoral dissertation). Retrieved from ProQuest Dissertations & Theses Global. (Order No. MQ72713)

Delagran, L., Vihstadt, C., & Evans, R. (2015). Aligning theory and design: The development of an online learning intervention to teach evidence-based practice for maximal reach. *Global Advances in Health and Medicine*, 4(5), 40–49.

Federal Bureau of Investigation & Penn State University. (2015). *We regret to inform you*. Retrieved from http://www.deathnotification.psu.edu/

Frymier, A. B., & Houser, M. L. (1998) Does making content relevant make a difference in learning? *Communication Research Reports, 15*(2), 121–129.

Gagne, R. (1977). *Conditions of learning* (3rd ed.). New York, NY: Holt, Rinehart and Winston.

Gorham, J., & Christophel, D. M. (1990). The relationship of instructors' use of humor in the classroom to immediacy and student learning. *Communication Education, 39*(1), 46–62.

Huett, J. B., Moller, L., Young, J., Bray, M., & Huett, K. C. (2008). Supporting the distant student: The effect of ARCS-based strategies on confidence and performance. *Quarterly Review of Distance Education, 9*(2), 113–126.

Johnson, R. (2012). *Community college first-year business student online course motivation* (Doctoral dissertation). Retrieved from ProQuest Dissertations & Theses Global. (Order No. 3513667)

Jokelova, A. (2013). ARCS motivational model. In A. Szakal (Ed.), *Eleventh IEEE international conference on emerging elearning technologies and applications (ICETA)* (pp. 189–194). New York, NY: Institute of Electrical and Electronics Engineers.

Keller, J. M. (1987). Development and use of the ARCS model of motivational design. *Journal of Instructional Development, 10*(3), 2–10.

Keller, J. M. (2010). *Motivational design for learning and performance*. New York, NY: Springer.

Knowles, M. S., Holton, E. F., III, & Swanson, R. A. (2015). *The adult learner: The definitive classic in adult education and human resource development* (8th ed.). New York, NY: Routledge.

Newby, T. J, Stepich, D. A., Lehman, J. D., Russell, J. D., & Ottenbreit-Leftwich, A. O. (2012). *Educational technology for teaching and learning* (4th ed.). Boston, MA: Pearson.

Pinchevsky-Font, T., & Dunbar, S. (2015). Best practices for online teaching and learning in health care related programs. *Internet Journal of Allied Health Sciences and Practice, 13*(1), 8.

Schartz, S. (2014). *The interrelationships of university student characteristics and the Keller ARCS motivation model in a blended digital literacy course* (Doctoral dissertation). Retrieved from http://krex.k-state.edu/dspace/handle/2097/18730

Taran, C. (2005). Motivation techniques in elearning. In P. Goodyear, D. G. Sampson, D. J.-T. Yang, Kinshuk, T. Okamoto, R. Hartley, & N.-S. Chen (Eds.), *Fifth IEEE international conference on advanced learning technologies (ICALT)* (pp. 617–619). New York, NY: Institute of Electrical and Electronics Engineers.

Thompson, L. (2016). Applying motivational design principles to create engaging online modules. In K. Thompson & B. Chen (Eds.), *Teaching online pedagogical repository*. Orlando, FL: University of Central Florida Center for Distributed Learning. Retrieved from https://topr.online.ucf.edu

Vygotsky, L. S. (1978). *Mind in society: The development of higher psychological processes*. Cambridge, MA: Harvard University Press.

Wanzer, M. B. (2010). An explanation of the relationship between instructor humor and student learning: Instructional humor processing theory. *Communication Education, 59*(1), 1–18.

Watkins, R. (2005). *75 e-learning activities*. San Francisco, CA: Wiley.

Polycom brings students, teachers and subjects together anywhere. Open up your classroom to an amazing world of content and cultures with the only end-to-end collaborative education solutions – Polycom, Inc.

Through interactive learning, an instructor can motivate and expose participants to people, places, and experiences without the traditional restrictions of time limitations or geographical barriers. Polycom's collaboration solutions are designed for educators by educators, providing a more human experience to collaborative communications enabling people to communicate and share ideas easily and intuitively through advanced voice, video and data conferencing solutions – with video clarity you can see, audio quality you can hear and ease-of-use you can feel. For more information, to obtain Grant Assistance and to access the most extensive video conferencing content database visit www.polycom.com/education.

POLYCOM

VIDEO   VOICE   DATA   WEB   TOGETHER, GREAT THINGS HAPPEN.

Try This

A Miniguide to Mentoring the Online Newbie Educator

Errol Craig Sull

Any so-called newbie to a course can use a bit of help; in the online environment this comes in one or more links that may contain faculty guides to teaching (at XXX school), to teaching specific courses, to a general guide of teaching students online, et cetera. But studies and anecdotal evidence have shown the use of a veteran faculty mentor can prove the most helpful, for he or she can give real-time input and feedback, be available for questions and help on a 24/7 basis, and establish a solid and positive connection that enhances the mentee's teaching skills and the mentee's role as an asset to the school.

Yet as with any advisor capacity there are certain approaches that should be taken to ensure the most positive outcome for the mentee, as mentor (and less formal "point person") assignments are given with the long-term goal of the mentee being an ongoing and contributing faculty member to the school. Here are suggestions to help make that happen:

Errol Craig Sull,
Adjunct Professor, Department of English,
Drexel University, P.O. Box 956,
Buffalo, NY 14207.
Telephone: (716) 871-1900.
E-mail: erroldistancelearning@gmail.com

- **Obtain as many basic details as possible from the assigning supervisor.** Going into a mentoring situation is more often than not meeting a stranger, and the more you know about that person the smoother and less stressful will go the first "Howdi-do!" You will certainly be given some info from the person assigning the mentee to you, but remember these questions (one or more may already be answered by the supervisor): What is this person's professional background? Has he/she taught other courses at the school and/or has this person taught/does the person teach at other schools? Is there anything special on which I should focus? How often would you like me to contact (e-mail and/or phone) this online educator?

- **First item: write an introductory and welcome letter to the mentee.** You will be given the mentee's e-mail address; be sure to write him or her immediately, enthusiastically welcoming the person to his or her new assignment, introducing yourself, and letting the individual know you are willing to help in any way possible—and that you are always open for questions. Also: be sure to mention the online environment; it either may be new to the person or you would want to ask if there is anything about the online environment for the course that still perplexes. Finally, add to the connection by sharing a bit about your personal life—hobbies, family, weather, et cetera—and asking the mentee to do the same. And if this is a first online course for the mentee share one of problems/challenges you first encountered: it's always nice for someone to know he or she is not alone in "having a first time"!

- **Create a list of the most important "to do" items in the class.** There may be basic items on this list—items that one would consider any online educator for your school ought to know—but that is okay; there is always the possibility that one or more of the items may not be known by the mentee, you can offer additional insights on one or more items of which the mentee had not considered, or info can be presented the mentee may have known but simply forgot. Additionally, include those items you believe are important to making the course successful—but do make sure these are more on the traditional side, that is, no whistles or bells … yet :).

- **Create a list of best practices and tips to excel in the class.** Here is where the so-called whistles and bells come into play: best practices—not those published or expected by the school (these would come under the previous bullet)—that you have created or adapted for use in your course that you believe are essential to having a successful course. Too, offer at least a few unorthodox or non-traditional teaching tips for the course you may have developed. Giving this to the mentee shows your solid interest in assisting him or her to do a fine job!

- **Set up a weekly phone call to chat about the mentees progress.** Speaking with the mentee is a great way to do that back-and-forth input/response that cannot be done via e-mail. Most important is hearing your tone of voice: enthusiastic and motivating just do not work as well in print! In addition, real-time comment can often lead to spur-of-the-moment thoughts from you or the mentee that might not happen in the slower exchange of e-mails. Finally, simply the act of talking with someone personalizes the relationship, allowing for a solid connection between mentor and mentee—and mentee to the school.

- **Send extra resources that have proven helpful.** This can be seen as the cherry on top of the mentoring: offering those little extras you have gathered for your courses—both in the general teaching of online courses and in the same subject being taught by the mentee—that you have found helpful for students. These can include newspaper and magazine articles, photos, puzzles, quotes, video and audio clips, and websites, as well as teaching strategies you have rated or adopted. One caution: don't send everything you have! You only want to give a few items, to both help and show your sincere concern for doing whatever you can to make the mentee's teaching experience a good one.

- **Always give feedback in a positive, motivating manner.** (NOTE: This suggestion is based on information only given by the mentee, that is, the mentor does not have access to the mentee's classroom.) This is one of those "no brainers," of course, but it's important to mention it, if only as a reminder. A mentor is not a lone contractor, but rather a representative of a university or college, and thus any feedback given to the mentee reflects on the school. The biggest piece of advice when it comes to feedback: look it over—word by word and tone of each comment—to be sure when it is submitted that feedback is not negative in words or tone, that vocabulary selected is politically correct and not disingenuous, and that it leaves one with the feeling of constructive criticism (if criticism is involved) and enthusiastic motivation. And when giving oral feedback just be sure the remarks are not spur-of-the-moment, but rather are thought through before offering them.
- **Give positive comments on the mentee's classroom (if applicable).** When the mentee's classroom is made available to you be sure to look it over for overall set-up of the classroom, remarks the mentee makes to students (including frequency), feedback in assignments (including timeliness of feedback), and use of all required course components (e.g., dropbox, discussion, quizzes, etc.). Additionally, see if there are areas that could be incorporated—optional for course use and not used by the mentee—that you have found are helpful.
- **Keep a record of all comments with the mentee.** Keeping a log of your substantive and meaningful comments (read: not "How's it going?" or "It's raining here!") to the mentee, as well as any from the mentee you believe to be insightful or meaningful to the mentee's ability in the classroom, is helpful for two reasons: [a] To help with future mentee assignments; [b] In case anything is questioned by your supervisor—or in the case of a complaint about you from the mentee. Also: as you think of new items or info you'd like to give a mentee or ways in which a situation could have been handled jot those down as well.
- **Write summaries—both required and not required.** Often, supervisors will require a summary of your experience with the mentee; but if not it is still advisable to send one: this shows your full completion of the assignment, as well as giving an overall assessment of the mentee's abilities—and any problems—in the classroom. Also: whether required or not, be sure the summary contains positive comments, when warranted. By the way: look over the notes you kept, include any quotes from the mentee you feel might be useful in the summary.

Remember: Watering seeds, giving fertilizer, and trimming when necessary result in plants that are strong, delightful, and pleasing—and contribute positively to the environment around them.

Ask Errol!

Errol Craig Sull

As we continue through 2016 there are new challenges, new developments, and new excitement in the field of distance learning. It is much like the stock market, with its ebbs and flows, but overall it is strong—a bull market that continues to grow. I'll continue to bring you responses to questions I receive so you can do your best in teaching online, and please do write me: your suggestions and inputs are welcome and encouraged.

Errol Craig Sull,
Adjunct Professor, Department of English, Drexel University, P.O. Box 956, Buffalo, NY 14207.
Telephone: (716) 871-1900.
E-mail: erroldistancelearning@gmail.com

This column's questions and my responses ...

This is a problem that I know plagues every online educator, and I keep hoping to read of some magic approach or the discovery of a previously unknown teaching strategy, but nothing is happening as I write you. My problem: no matter the efforts I put in I continue to have some students who remain on my roster as being active members in my classes, but they have not showed their involvement in any component of the course. This means they do not turn in assignments, they do not participate in discussions, they do not respond to my e-mails. Do you have any suggestions? Thank you.

You are right, of course: the problem you describe is systemic, and has been a challenge since distance learning was first birthed, precomputer in the 19th century and postcomputer from the 1960s. And while this ongoing hiccup in online learning shows no sign of going away soon, advances have been made that minimize the number of no-shows. As you do not mention what approaches you have tried what I offer may have already been explored by you, but here are pedagogies that have proven most successful: (a) Call the person; so often a call can create that personal connection that a no-show needs. Also, you may learn of a serious problem that has occupied the person so much the course has been on a secondary level of importance, and thus you may find a way to help that person around the problem so he or she can continue in the course. (b) Learn what you can about the background of a no-show: there might be info in the course, but also ask your supervisor and the no-show's advisor; when you get this information contact the no-show, using the info to better explain the course's importance and to better connect with the student. (c) Contact the student's advisor, and ask that person to contact the no-show; also, the advisor might have some info you do not that might prove helpful in getting the person to be an active part of the course. (d) If you learn of something that is not private about the no-show (for example, current employment, hobby interests, etc.) create a discussion thread that somehow connects to one part of this info, then send an e-mail to the email letting him/her know—and how you would appreciate it if the person would lead it off. Nothing is foolproof, of course, but each of these has resulted in getting no-shows alive in courses!

Errol, thanks so much for the info you have offered over the years—much of it has helped me become a better online educator! Now, I have a specific question that partially is the result of suggestions you have given in your columns. In some of the online faculty forums I have contributed a few mentions of teaching strategies I do in my classes, and often I receive e-mails from faculty asking me for details on how I do this or that. Certainly, I want to share—but how much? I feel that if I give everything I have created it is no longer unique to me, that what are now fairly unique approaches to teaching in my department will simply become same old same old. Of course, I also not want to appear stingy, and in every department there is a "all for one and one for all" approach to faculty members. What is your opinion?

First, thanks very much for the nice words; it is always a pleasure to learn my columns are proving helpful to other distance educators! As for your conundrum, at first it may seem like a "sticky wicket," but you can respond to each colleague in a manner that both protects what is yours—so to speak—while also giving enough to satisfy even the most "Help me!"-starved faculty member. What you do is to give a basic outline of your approach, then tell your colleagues it is up to them to fill in the rest based on the specifics of their students and subject, as well as their own thoughts on what would work. And in addition to you being thought of as a really good team player it can also help you in another way: end your e-mails asking each person to get back to you with what he or she developed; those who do might offer you an approach you had not previously considered.

What has me confused is a staple of every online course: that first letter, the so-called "Welcome Letter." I've been teaching online for 1 year, and it seems that everything I think students ought to know before starting my classes I toss into my welcome letter, but when I read it over it is really, really long! Trying to look at this as if I were a student it could appear intimidating, and I do not really know if my students read the entire letter or if they do read it how much of the info really stays with them. Is there a formula of some sort for writing the "perfect" welcome letter?

Without question that "Welcome to my course!" announcement—and often also usually sent out as a group e-mail—is crucial, for it sets the tone for what students can expect in the class (read: your personality and teaching style) and what the professor considers most important in the course. And as you mention, having such a letter that is too long can translate into one not read or items in the letter glossed over. While each such letter is subjective to each online educator there are some guidelines that should be the architecture of any welcome letter: (a) the letter should begin with a friendly and enthusiastic paragraph that welcomes the students, offers your excitement for teaching the course, and tells students you will give them everything they need to do well—and all they must give in return is effort; (b) the next paragraph should mention the bullets that follow are especially important to the course, but other announcements have been posted that expand on additional components of the course (this way you are, in essence, dividing your welcome letter into easily digestible bites); (c) use color, bolding, italics, and highlighting for important points—this not only emphasizes their seriousness but breaks up the black-on-white, black-on-white, black-on-white that can become boring; (d) end the letter by letting students know you really want them to succeed, you look forward to working together, and you are always open for their questions and comments (via e-mail, of course, but also phone if an option). Note: Do not let that welcome letter simply sit there, to be forgotten after a couple of days; refer to one or more of its contents throughout the course; this spotlights the welcome letter's importance.

I teach science courses, Errol, and to illustrate how a theory or principle or piece of information can be used in everyday life I often show the students a movie or two throughout the course. The students really like this, of course, but recently a supervisor pointed out to me that I should make better use of the films I show so they better integrate with the course material, but never offered any meaningful suggestions. Can you give me some ideas?

This is a question I have had tossed my way in different formats: not only using movies but also music, TV shows, and poetry/short stories/plays. Each presents a golden opportunity to expand students' critical thinking while also highlighting the overall course subject or areas of the subject. I have used movies on many occasions for American Lit courses I have taught, and integrating them with the course material proves very helpful to the students' understanding of the material while also tickling their thought processes. Try these: (a) if students are given something to read, then see a movie based on that reading material have them do a short essay that notes the differences between the two, asking which works better and why; (b) does the material presented in the movie—that relates directly to your course—realistically reflect on what the material could do in "real life," and if not why not/and if yes how could the students see this material helping in the future? (c) in looking at the movie what makes the material more exciting than what it appears to be in the course—and what new insights have students gained on the material in the movie they did not get from the course? [d] could the students see ways the material could be used in a different way in the movie—and how? Why do they think it was not used in that way? What might be the outcome of a scene, a character, or the overall theme if it was incorporated in this unused manner? Each of these makes a movie an important segment of a course, for it expands the materials role in the course and in the outside world, that is, the material studied becomes real and pragmatic.

Remember: A pride of lions, a herd of elephants, a pod of dolphins: they learn from each other, and thus are stronger and wiser to teach their offspring to survive and prosper.

And Finally ... *continued from page 80*

One commonality between classroom flipping and single-concept teaching is the use of motion media. Film, the classic motion medium, has inherent disadvantages: cost, training, distribution, duplication, and equipment, all which have become irrelevant in the day of smart phones, free editing software, easy-to-use storage locations, and digital media.

Thus, it is possible to take the best of these ideas—flipping course content by using short, motion-media presentations, and organizing the media into a series of related and often sequential single-concept lessons. The unit-module-topic approach to course organization provides structure to this approach. The building block of instruction is the single concept—or single topic. Topics/concepts are organized into modules, which in turn are collected into course units.

Certainly it is a good idea to use short, "one-idea" videos as homework, either created locally or found online. Course content is partially delivered by digital media, then regular and substantive interaction can be made available in chats, threaded discussions, and synchronous videoconferences.

And finally, remember back to that great teacher from high school or college—he or she probably identified key ideas and visualized them in images, even words, organized sequentially. The approaches have not changed as much as the tools.

And Finally ...

Flipping, Single Concepts, and Video
So Many New Ideas—Or Are They?

Michael Simonson

Flipping a classroom refers to recording a class lecture so students watch and listen at home to free up time in the classroom for discussions. What a popular idea (a silly one, too); teachers have always assigned homework, and then used class time instructor for explanation, review, amplification, and questions.

Michael Simonson, Editor, *Distance Learning,* and Program Professor, Programs in Instructional Technology and Distance Education, Fischler School of Education, Nova Southeastern University, 1750 NE 167 St., North Miami Beach, FL 33162. Telephone: (954) 262-8563. E-mail: simsmich@nsu.nova.edu

Of course some instructors still lecture. And, lecturing is okay, probably more so for traditional teachers than for distance educators. Today, it would be unheard of for a distance teacher to have a 50-minute presentation with little or no student interaction, yet flipped classroom advocates seem to promote recording lectures.

The next old idea with a new level of popularity is the single-concept lesson; this approach, although classic, is a great one. Single-concept teaching is a product of the mastery learning movement of the 1960s and 1970s, and is a technique of teaching that uses the single concept as the building block of instruction. Generally a single-concept lesson is a relatively short 3–5 minute mediated presentation of an idea with a clear introduction, body, and conclusion.

The epitome of the single-concept lesson of the mastery learning generation was the film loop, a 3–4 minute motion picture showing a key idea such as mitosis in biology or the definition of median in statistics. Today, Youtube and Vimeo are loaded with single-concept lessons. When single-concept lessons are part of a series and can be distributed or pushed to interested viewers as a series they are called podcasts.

... continues on page 79